Terry McMillan

The Unauthorized Biography

Terry
McMillan

The Unauthorized Biography

Diane Patrick

St. Martin's Press ≋ New York

THOMAS DUNNE BOOKS.
An imprint of St. Martin's Press.

Library of Congress Cataloging-in-Publication Data

Patrick, Diane.
    Terry McMillan : the unauthorized biography / Diane Patrick.—
1st U.S. ed.
      p.   cm.
    ISBN 0-312-20032-3
    1. McMillan, Terry. 2. Women novelists, American—20th
    century—Biography. 3. Afro-American women novelists—
    Biography.
  I. Title.
PS3563.C3868Z86   1999
813'.54—dc21
[B]   99-23849
                                           CIP

First Edition: September 1999

10 9 8 7 6 5 4 3 2 1

Acknowledgments

Warmest acknowledgments of indebtedness go to my colleagues and friends at *Publishers Weekly* for their good-natured support, especially Ingrid Chevannes, Daisy Maryles, Judy Quinn, Calvin Reid, Esther Reid, and Isabell Taylor, with extra special thanks to Gary Ink (the king of information!) for your untiring assistance, and Jeff Zaleski for your *damn* good advice. To the wonderful folks in Port Huron, especially Allison Arnold, Eulalio Briones, Alex Crittenden, Marilyn Dunn, Mary Goschnik, Spurgeon Harvey, Debbie Lepley, Marguerite Stanley, and Steve Williams, for sharing valuable materials, connections, and memories. To Bill Banks, Manie Barron, Marie Brown, Grace Edwards, Lawrence Kessenich, D. T. Max, Rebecca Johnson Melvin, Ishmael Reed, Lisa Shipley, Wendy Smith, Clyde Taylor, and Sarah Elizabeth Wright, for helping the facts come to life. To Jerry Oppenheimer (O king of the genre!) and Paul Colford, for listening and sharing—you guys are fabulous. To my college English professors Elizabeth Nunez and Barbara Summers, whose advice is still as priceless today as it was twenty-five years ago—when we were all infants! (Isn't it a small world?) To Toni Banks and Carol Taylor, my personal angels, I love youse to bits. To my dear friend and wisewoman Toni "It's time to quit your job" Roberts, whose valuable les-

Acknowledgments

sons have charged—*and* changed—my life. To all the journalists and behind-the-scenes angel-helpers who preferred anonymity, but generously helped to fill in the gaps. Of course to my agent Madeleine Morel, who started all this in the first place, and my editor, Kristen Nardullo. And even to Terry McMillan, with whose help it would have been easier . . . but probably not as much fun!

Terry McMillan

The Unauthorized Biography

Foreword

What's "Unauthorized" Got to Do with It?

I don't know why you people don't wait until I'm dead.
—Terry McMillan

It was maybe late 1990, early 1991. On my way to the bargain section of some New York City bookstore—I can't remember which—and minding my own business, I was sidetracked when the paperback edition of Terry McMillan's *Disappearing Acts* flew into my hands. I had never heard of Terry McMillan. Didn't even know if it was a boy Terry or a girl Terry.

And this, let me add, happened in the regular section of the bookstore, a section that was virtually alien territory to me. Full price was my enemy—as a long time paralegal who was in the early stages of a freelance writing career, rarely could I afford to buy books at full price—and thus the bargain section was my second home. But my journeys to Bargainville were nothing to sneeze at: They had helped me bulk up the shelves of my per-

1

sonal library with reference, biography, black history, and black classics. Contemporary fiction, though, was a genre I rarely bought. I found that borrowing it from the library was more economical.

Whether I bought it or borrowed it, my standards for whether I would read a work of fiction were very simple since I'm neither an academician nor a literary expert; I'm just Diane Q. Public. For me, a book has to pass the First-Sentence Test. Which is, If the first sentence can grab me, I'll give the book a play.

So there I was with *Disappearing Acts* in my hands. I opened the book and read the first sentence.

Well, as you know, the first sentence of *Disappearing Acts* was written from a man's point of view. This man, Franklin, was complaining—no, more like ranting and raving, with *plenty* of good old-fashioned cursing—about how women always got serious once they got "some good lovin'," and how the last thing he wanted was to get serious about some woman, and on and on. I busted out laughing right there in the store. Whoever you are, Terry, I thought to myself, you got my money today! I went to the counter, and gave up my hard-earned nine dollars—plus New York City tax—for the little book with the black, purple, and turquoise cover.

This book also needled me about something I wanted to write myself someday. I am fortunate enough to have close male friends, and we constantly and freely discuss relationships, families, careers, sex, love, you name it. Their stories are fascinating and often inspiring; yet when I suggest they share these feelings with other men—in diary form, maybe?—they hem and haw, and then I threaten to write their stories myself, in a male voice. So *Disappearing Acts* fascinated me also because here was a sista-girl who had done it already; my purchase of her book was not only for enjoyment, but to illustrate the You Snooze, You Lose rule—and to rub my own face in it, so to speak.

A little while later, I bought—again at full price—*Breaking Ice,* the anthology of black writing which was edited by Terry McMillan. With its almost five dozen short stories by contemporary black writers, *Breaking Ice* seemed like a good book to have in my reference library—especially considering that there were not too many of those kinds of books around.

Now I had *two* books with Terry McMillan's name on their spines.

And then suddenly, her name was all over the place. When her third novel, *Waiting to Exhale,* was published in 1992, women black and white were raving over its no-holds-barred storyline—set in our time and in an American city—of four middle-class black girlfriends and their problems with men. I broke down and put my name on the public library's reserve list and patiently waited umpteen weeks for a copy to become available.

After reading *Waiting to Exhale,* my reaction was "Uh, I guess I must not really be black" because I did not know, had never known, and did not ever want to know, any women who were unable to *function* owing to not having a man! Sure, I could understand pining for a man, and being in love, and wanting to be in love, and being frustrated, and all that. But that's where my understanding stopped.

Obviously, I was in a tiny minority because the book sold, and sold, and sold. Sistas was buying, and buying, and buying it. Forget my one humble little opinion, baby. When something sells, like it or not, in our capitalist society, it's a message no one can ignore: There's something about it that compels people to buy it. So that's when sista Terry's name became a household word, and now that publishers had a taste of how well Terry's books sold, the world of black readers and black writers changed. For black writers, Terry's topic opened the door to a whole new genre to explore: the "girlfriend" novel. And of course the success of the subsequent movie version of *Waiting to Exhale* made Terry even huger.

By that time, my freelance writing career was a decade old, and I had left the legal profession to devote full time and energies to writing. But I was never the kind of writer who wrote first and then tried to sell what I wrote. No, I was what I referred to as a "hired pen:" Editors and publishers called me and gave me assignments. And what I did best was write about people, which has been a lifelong interest. I interviewed musicians for entertainment magazine articles, album liner notes, and press materials. I interviewed legal professionals for legal articles. I wrote biographical entries on writers, scientists, and musicians for reference books. I wrote children's books on government and African American history and biographies of figures such as Martin Luther King, Jr., Coretta King, Barbara Jordan, Toni Morrison, Walter Dean Myers, and Colin Powell. But as I got older and better, the money wasn't proportionate to the time and energy I expended.

In other words, after ten years, I decided enough with the children's books already! It was time for me to graduate.

I picked up the phone, called my agent, and told her that I now wanted to write adult biographies.

A few weeks later, she called and asked if I would be interested in writing a biography of Terry McMillan.

And that's how I came to write this book.

As tough as Terry McMillan may appear to be, she is very sensitive about her acceptance among the established writing community, and has lamented that some of the more successful black female writers have not acknowledged her, despite her having "gone out of my way to show respect for them." She is especially hurt by the author Alice Walker, who, Terry felt, once dissed her when they met briefly.

Which suggests that she would be happy, as both an author and a member of the publishing community, to have her biography written. That she would at least be courteous if she met the biographer, and pleased to see that the biographer was a black woman with many things in common with her. That if she did not want to cooperate or contribute, she would at least give the biographer her blessing and provide access to important research sources like family and friends.

But NO.

I must confess that although I did own all of Terry's books by the time I took this assignment, I had never met her (don't like lines and crowds) and somehow managed to miss all her appearances on television. But I knew that her life was pretty much an open book, excuse the pun: She'd done countless interviews and she had been pretty candid in every one. Every word she wrote, everywhere, had some strong biographical elements. Still, as a researcher with a no-nonsense work ethic, I prefer to get my information from the source whenever possible. Especially in an important biography like this! So as soon as I signed the contract, I wrote Terry a letter in care of her agent and introduced myself, told her about the project, and asked if she would care to participate.

Now mind you, I was under no obligation to inform or advise Terry that I was doing this; I did it as a courtesy because I have that work ethic thing and, well, I'm a nice person. Besides, I have worked with and interviewed celebrities for years, and not one of them has *ever* complained about my methods or my work; quite the opposite has been the case, because I have proven that I can be trusted with the words that are shared with me.

My reason for contacting Terry was not that I wanted her to spend weeks with me and my tape recorder, giving me a blow-by-blow story of her life. That could potentially lead to my saying exactly what she wanted me to say, which would lead to the thing reading like a giant, kissy-ass press release, or an "as told to" book, which I was not under contract to write. (I am reminded of another author who wrote an unauthorized biography of a famous person. The contract—which is between the author and the publisher, mind you—allowed the *subject* to check the manuscript for accuracy. When that time came, ego took over, and the subject sent the manuscript to friends, relatives, and by the time it was all over, had marked it up mercilessly and returned it to the author. Who needs that?) But neither was I under contract to write a "hatchet-job," which was just fine because I am not that type of writer and Terry's was not that type of life. Besides, my preliminary research was not uncovering any deep, dark secrets. My intention was to write a book that showed how a black girl, from a town that blacks rarely get out of, became a huge success as a writer.

Less than a week after sending my letter, I got back a hand-written card. Not from Terry, not from Terry's agent, but from Terry's assistant—informing me that Terry was busy touring and writing a screenplay and that she would have no time for interviews.

Fine. I was on my own.

I began my research.

A few weeks later, there was a message on my answering machine. A husky, gravelly voice emitted. "Diane Patrick, this is Terry McMillan. I'd like to know who your publisher is and why you guys are writing an unauthorized biography of *me*. Would somebody please tell me this? I'd really appreciate it. My number is————. I'd sorta like to know the nature of this biography, you know? Maybe if I have some skeletons in my closet you might be able to help me with 'em. Thank you."

Yes! I thought. That last sentence gave me hope. Girlfriend is gonna talk to me, we'll become friends because we have so much in common, and this is going to be the biography of doom. Accurate, detailed, and everything.

I called back and left a message thanking her for her call and inviting her to call me again anytime.

The very next day, I learned that Terry was going to be in New York City the following week, signing paperback copies of her latest book, *How Stella Got Her Groove Back,* at Barnes and Noble. This was excellent news: Here was a chance for me to show my face, for her to look at me and see that I was a nice, honest, sweet, unpretentious, nonthreatening person—in short, the best person on earth to write her biography. (And a soul sista, too! What's not to like?) Yes, even before I opened my mouth, my innocent brown eyes would assure her.

Oh yes, I was confident. So, I boogied on down to what would be my first book-toting, line-waiting experience.

I got there two hours early (long enough to sit in one of the cushy chairs and read *The Kiss* by Kathryn Harrison). By the time I finished it, the Terry line was beginning to form, and I took my place on it, carrying my own copies of *Stella* and *Disappearing Acts.* The line moved quickly, and in fifteen minutes I was in sight of the velvet ropes, the unsmiling faces of the assistants whose job it was to open your book to the page on which she would sign, and then . . . her! She was wearing a black knit dress under a colorfully striped long knit duster, with her hair all up in a topknot of crinkly curls, sitting at a long table covered with a white cloth, signing away. In a few seconds, I was face-to-face with my subject—for the very first time. I laid the books down, then introduced myself.

She looked up in my face as soon as she heard my name. (Girlfriend has a great memory for detail.) I expected her to smile and say she was glad to meet me. Maybe we could go out for a drink after. (Oops, I mean coffee.)

But I woke up fast. "You're the one who's writing the unauthorized biography!" she growled, without smiling, in a tone that suggested that her next sentence would be "Guards! Throw this woman out!" (Or, in street-speak, "Get this bitch outta here!")

"Yes," I said, stunned. "I just wanted to introduce myself and let you know that I'm available anytime you want to talk. I'll be happy to talk with you."

She signed one of my books, then the other (limit was two), grumbling. "I don't know why you people don't wait until I'm *dead*," she muttered, without looking at me. Then she stood up to her full height—about five feet seven—to greet someone who had been allowed behind the table to talk to her, and the line-minders were ushering the next person up, and it was time for me to mosey on along. But now I was getting a little pissed. Feeling dissed. So I said sarcastically, "Well, I'm just a poor black girl from the Bronx, trying to write a book. You know how to reach me." And I left, puzzled. What had I done to her? Was this how Alice Walker had made *her* feel? Was this her way of recycling that alleged Alice Walker diss? I thought having your feelings hurt made you a kinder, gentler person. Hmm.

I met Terry once more after that, at a fund-raising dinner party for the Yaddo artist's colony at which she was a guest of honor. By then, it appeared to me that she had instructed her family and friends not to speak with me and was frustrating my research attempts. This time, I was able to get in a few more sentences, trying to reassure her that I wanted the book to be as fair and accurate as possible, and that her participation would only advance that cause. But again, despite my attempts to get her to relax, she seemed more and more threatened by the idea of the project. All I could get from her was that the idea of a biography just scared her for some reason, although I knew that she had nothing all that embarrassing in her past, certainly no more than the rest of us. For all her protests, though, she either could not or would not express any understandable reason for her opposition to the project—and she clearly had no intentions of warming up to me.

In one last attempt to break through, I called Molly Friedrich, Terry's agent. Molly listened sympathetically, and provided her explanation for Terry's attitude: Because Terry's very private and from the heart, she feels put-upon in general. And when you feel that people are making a living off you, you start getting really protective. I nevertheless prevailed upon Molly to speak to Terry on my behalf, and she was kind enough to agree to try. But Molly came back, sounding exasperated, to tell me that Terry was "just adamant. She's in a state, she is very upset that this biography is being written. She doesn't feel that her life is important enough or that her body of work is large enough. She doesn't want a book written where she would have to come out and defend herself," Molly said, adding, "she had that *tone*. I didn't even say anything."

It made no sense to me that Terry wouldn't realize her own importance by this point in her life. But it did make sense to me that I was wasting my time even trying to coax her into participating. So I sent Terry a silent prayer and a blessing and kept on with the project, obstacles and all. I mean, I'm a professional—and I had a deadline to meet.

Terry McMillan is well educated, very resourceful, and intelligent. She can go anywhere and do anything, can converse and debate in any setting. Still, she can leave you with a feeling of Damn, what did I do to her? She craves love, values her friendships, and is said to be loyal to her friends, but she can be caustic to everyone, friend or not, at a moment's notice. She has a tough manner, she is never completely soft or gentle. She always seems to be expecting to be disappointed, with a do-unto-others-but-do-it-first attitude, as if she has been too often burned, possibly by her experiences with an abusive stepfather and disappointments in her own romances. She acts as if she feels obligated to protect herself. You can ask her the most innocuous question and if she didn't hear you, she'll say "What?" in a truly challenging tone of voice. You have to be very thick-skinned to communicate with her and not feel that she's pissed off at you.

For ten years now, Terry McMillan has opened up to every journalist and television interviewer in creation. If there are any remaining secrets in her life, I couldn't unearth them for *this* biography.

The performance of Terry McMillan's books—that is, the way they've sold and the reaction they've sparked—has changed the way the publishing industry regards both black authors and black readers. Because as hard as it may be to believe, Before Terry

(B. T.) publishers assumed that black people did not buy books. But once *Waiting to Exhale* sold over 700,000 hardcover copies and over three million more in paperback, the publishing industry was forced to admit that books by black authors *can* sell, that black readers *do* exist, and that black people *do* spend their dollars on books.

Almost as astounding as those numbers is the fact that the publishing industry had to be *forced* to believe all this.

Who has bought Terry McMillan's novels? Mostly black women who were thirsty and hungry to see their lives, their lifestyles, their words, their issues between the covers of a novel.

Did she plan to become this phenomenon? Probably not. As all writers do, she just wanted to write. But Terry McMillan had two additional powers. She had ambition, and she had business savvy. These were no accident: She made it her business to learn about both the *craft* of writing and the *business* of writing, and she put herself in places where she could learn these things. And she paid attention to what she learned.

She sure was paying attention when somebody said "Write what you know," the advice every novice writer hears. Because what Terry McMillan knows—and lives—is the life of the contemporary, urban, middle-class black woman. That is, the black career woman who lives in a city and is struggling with all the questions, answers, trappings, friends, and dilemmas that go with that life.

The other thing Terry knows about—that she is *fascinated* by—is the ups and downs of relationships. Her first novel, *Mama* (1987), and her next novel (to date unpublished), *A Day Late and a Dollar Short,* were inspired by her own mother's relationships with her five children as well as the men in her life. *Disappearing Acts* (1990), *Waiting to Exhale* (1992), and *How Stella Got Her Groove Back* (1997) were inspired by Terry's relationships with men. Pretty simple, hmm?

Maybe. But while anyone can write, it is something else to elevate it from a hobby to a serious craft. To find, and surround yourself with, kindred spirits who ask "What are you writing now?" instead of "Why don't you take that test next week for that post office job?" To adjust, sometimes contort, your lifestyle so that you can have the time and a place to refine and practice your craft undisturbed. And after all that, it is something else again to take yourself and your work *out* of that safe cocoon, to find and meet the right people who can help you polish your work. To get published. To earn a living off your talent. Yes, it takes time, commitment, hard work, patience, and perseverance.

Even for those who are independently wealthy and who don't need to hold down a nine-to-five job, becoming a writer who actually makes a *living* off writing is a struggle. For a black girl from a small town in Michigan where one of the highest aspirations was to work in the local automobile factory, a writing career was certainly not an obvious option.

But there are some creatures who have a curiosity. An impatience. An orneriness, if you will. These creatures are destined to break away from the herd and roam in pastures previously uncharted. And Terry was one such creature. She broke away from the herd—and that is why we know her name.

Whether you like her writing or not, whether you like her

personality or not, you have to give Terry McMillan props for creating her own reality. Her story is not so much a story of luck and serendipity as a story of traveling a path that you can't see, but want to reach the end of anyway. It's also a story of hard work: She didn't take no for an answer when someone said, "Okay, we're publishing your first novel, but sorry, we don't have a big budget to promote first novels by unknown writers, so don't expect it to sell." She simply promoted the thing herself—so well that it sold out its first printing before it was even published.

Why do some creatures break away from the herd? Some say it's astrology: Look at the stars the person was born under, the date, the time, the season, and there will be signs in those aspects. Others say it's an ancestor who was a kindred spirit, or the return of such an ancestor. Still others would surmise that it's the environment: in Terry's case, an abusive and alcoholic father and stepfather, a boring small town, no local role models. She just had to break free. Yes, but why Terry, and not the rest of the herd?

Everyone has an opinion about Terry McMillan. These opinions cover a huge range, of course, with something for everyone: Her books are great. She tells *our* stories. She's the greatest writer of our time. *Great?* Are you kidding? She's not literary enough. She's not black enough. She's not political enough. She's not militant enough. She curses too much (dammit). She's writing pap. She's writing pop. She disses the brothas. She's vibrant. She's forceful. She's animated. She's got presence. *Presence?* Are you kidding? She's got a stink attitude. She's too street. She's too coarse. She's too rough in person. Her sentences were too long *(Stella)*. Her characters were too neurotic *(Exhale)*. Her ex-boyfriend felt that a certain male character *(Disappearing Acts)* was too much like him, so he sued her for four and a half million bucks for defamation of character. And on and on. Depends on who you talk to. For everyone you ask, you get a different opinion.

But does Terry care? Nah. Those who break away from the herd automatically don't care. They can withstand being criticized. Sometimes from as near as their own family, and so criticism either makes them tougher or destroys them. So just as Terry has no frame of reference from which to write about the homeboy-from-the-'hood experience, she has no frame of reference for enduring guilt trips from those who wish she would write what they wish she would write. And what's more fun is, she can laugh all the way to the bank—because she has what every author prays to have: people reading (and buying) her books. Not to mention Hollywood making those books into movies.

Yet, for all her success and for all the criticism, Terry McMillan doesn't spend her time looking down her nose at writing that's different from hers. Her feeling is that writing is a gift, and it must be cultivated and respected and appreciated. She appreciates the classics, by authors of all colors and backgrounds. She will never diss a genre, an author, a topic. She takes the time to teach writing to the next generation of young novice writers. She gives thousands (and thousands) of dollars at a time to programs and individuals who need education and assistance. She writes how-to articles about the craft of writing. She is happy that young black writers are getting published. She writes blurbs (phrases of endorsements) for the books of promising young black authors. She is genuinely committed to the writing life, all that goes with it, and all who come behind her.

1

Early Years

Some children are born with their own destiny in mind, their path is laid out in front of them already—only you can't see it.

From *A Day Late and a Dollar Short* by Terry McMillan
(work-in-progress version)

Port Huron was . . . a depressing little place to live. I fled Port Huron and I don't have any regrets about it.

—Terry McMillan

M*ama,* Terry McMillan's first novel, is set in the fictitious town of Point Haven, Michigan, and is based on Terry's own growing-up years in the real town of Port Huron, Michigan. There is a disclaimer on its front pages: "This book is a work of fiction. Names, characters, places, and incidents are either the product of the author's imagination or are used fictitiously. Any resemblance to actual events or locales or persons, living or dead, is entirely coincidental."

Disclaimer or not, *Mama* is so transparently fictionalized that one can get a pretty good dose of Terry McMillan autobiography by reading it. Anyone who lived in Port Huron's black community could easily recognize the people and places mentioned; in fact, anyone who *didn't* live there could use parts of the book as a guide when visiting.

Of course, only Port Huronites know everything for sure, and then there are certain things only the McMillan family would know (and these must have pushed some buttons because one of Terry's aunts reportedly stopped speaking to her as a result!); but still, much is obvious.

The most obvious thing is that Terry McMillan did not think very highly of the town she grew up in.

The quotation that Terry chose for the beginning of *Mama* expresses this in a very subtle way, best understood in retrospect—just like life. It is from the poem "When I Have Reached the Point of Suffocation" by Gerald Stern:

> It takes years to learn how to look at the destruction
> of beautiful things;
>
> to learn how to leave the place
> of oppression;
>
> and how to make your own regeneration
> out of nothing.

"Out of this community? Out of Port Huron, out of Port Huron in the sixties? Black kids in Port Huron could *not* get out. No. Terry was not supposed to make it! It's tough enough now because the kids are not motivated."

That was the passionate response of Alex Crittenden, principal of the Cleveland School in Port Huron, Michigan, when asked why it was such a big deal that Terry McMillan had left that community and become a famous author. This conversation took place in 1997, over forty years after five-year-old Terry began running down the halls of that tiny elementary school.

There are some people who are born in a certain place. Their families live there, they make friends there, go to school there, work there, marry someone from there, raise children there, and die there—all without having seen what is just around the bend, or in the next town, city, or state.

It may be by choice, this insularity: They may truly, simply, love the community. Or it may be lack of opportunity: No one drives up in their car, toots the horn, and says "Hey, let's go around the bend (or to the next town, city, or state)." It may be because no one they know has ever left. It may be that every-day life is the focus, and there is no time to think of, or imagine, or be concerned about, an Elsewhere.

Still, there is always one: one ornery, disobedient, eccentric soul who can't stop looking at the horizon and wondering, just what *is* beyond that? Or who sees a picture in a book, magazine, or on television, of Someplace Else, and wonders, what's it like there? Or hears or reads a story of an adventurous traveler and thinks, hmm, wonder what it's like to roam.

Who knows? Maybe ornery, disobedient, eccentric souls are

born that way, with a curiosity, a kind of wanderlust. Zora Neale Hurston, another such child, put it this way in her 1942 biography *Dust Tracks on a Road:*

> *One of the most serious objections to me was that having nothing, I still did not know how to be humble. A child in my place ought to realize I was lucky to have a roof over my head and anything to eat at all. And from their point of view, they were right, from mine, my stomach pains were the least of my sufferings. I wanted what they could not conceive of.*

As early as anyone can remember, Terry McMillan always wanted to leave Port Huron. The first-born daughter, she had an uncanny sense that there was more than this, somewhere, and always looked toward the horizon. Growing up in a small town where nothing much happened, that was the best thing she could have ever done.

Alex Crittenden is a sharp-dressing, friendly, gregarious, no-nonsense powerhouse of a black man, of average height and build, and high standards. He has been principal of the Cleveland School for only a few years, but he lovingly runs this one-story rust-colored brick school as if it were his own home. Still, he points out that aspirations of the black kids in the town are not all that different today than they were forty years ago.

"Which is why," Terry herself once told a reporter for her hometown newspaper, "it amazes me that people stay here. There is *so* much more these people can do than work for Detroit Edison and the phone company. If . . . parents don't motivate [their kids], then they're going to be stuck here for the rest of their lives, doing nothing."

Maybe Crittenden's vantage point is more objective, as he is not from Port Huron. A dedicated principal who is loved by the students and teachers, he hands out candy to the kids and lets the teachers paint and decorate the classrooms, bathrooms, corridors, and lounge areas as if they were their own homes. He corrects the children's language, patiently urging them to convert a "Can I have some candy" to "May I have some candy, please?" Still, he sees the inertia in the black community of Port Huron, and he tries every day to do something about it, to maybe inspire one more Terry McMillan.

On the map of the United States, three of the Great Lakes—Erie, Michigan, and Huron—have carved the state of Michigan into what resembles a mitten. The city of Port Huron is located at the top of what is locally known as the thumb of that mitten. With Canada right next door, Michigan's two closest crossing points into that country are at Port Huron and Detroit. Thus, during slavery, Michigan was a favorite place for fugitive slaves to cross into the "promised land" of Canada.

Port Huron is sixty miles northeast of Detroit, the city where many abolitionists and antislavery activists did their work during slavery, and, hundreds of years later, where the Motown sound was born. A pretty city, with lots of trees and grass, Port Huron's waterways include Lake Huron, the St. Clair River, and the Black River. Across the St. Clair River is the Canadian city of Sarnia, Ontario. So it's really a scenic place: trees, grass, water.

The official tourism materials tell you that Port Huron's most famous citizen was Thomas Alva Edison, inventor of the electric lightbulb, sound-recording device, and motion picture projector. Edison lived there with his family from 1854, when he was seven years old, until 1863; his first experiments with electricity and chemistry were done in his basement laboratory there. To make money, he sold candy and newspapers on the train that then ran between Port Huron and Detroit.

Not surprisingly, there is nothing in the official tourism materials about the city's black community. It is fortunate, then, that the task of compiling this information was undertaken by Mrs. Marguerite Stanley, a longtime black resident of Port Huron. Mrs. Stanley, a former counselor in Port Huron's high schools, formed her memories and research into an unofficial history of black Port Huron, which was published as a twenty-eight-page booklet in 1977. Now retired, Mrs. Stanley—a delightful lady with a melodious voice who generously punctuates her conversation with "honey" and "sweetheart"—paints a richly textured picture of black Port Huron, to which she was brought in 1924 as a baby.

"In my childhood," she remembers, "the town was close-knit enough that everybody knew each other. Even if a new car came down the street, you automatically knew somebody had a visitor."

In her historical account entitled *From Whence We Came,* Stanley explains that until the late 1950s, the black community in Port Huron was concentrated in an area called South Park, which was roughly ten blocks long by about seven blocks wide and located well south of the downtown area.

"As far as employment was concerned," remembers Mrs. Stanley, "we had some factories at the time. Quite a few people had to go out of town for work. The primary places they worked were New Haven, which was one hour away, Detroit, one and a half hours away, and Mount Clemens, one hour and twenty minutes away. Not everyone had a car, but people pooled.

"There weren't too many opportunities in town," she continued. "Not for anybody, and certainly not for us as blacks. In town, most of the work that blacks did was in service: The women worked in private homes. There was a main street, which had hardware stores, Sperry's, a clothing store, Kresge's five and ten, Spike's Furniture Store. There were a few, a very few, blacks who clerked in the stores or worked as elevator operators at the banks. But for the most part those who had what I would consider economically sustaining jobs worked in the factories or worked in the automobile plants in the Detroit area." For a time, Mrs. Stanley herself worked in New Haven in the foundry of a Chrysler supplier plant. "Dirty, dirty, dirty," she says, "but I made money!"

As in any neighborhood, the blacks in Port Huron created a thriving network to provide goods and services for their community. Some started businesses in their homes. In her book, Mrs. Stanley paints almost a living picture of those days: There were barbers and hairdressers, such as Charles "Cy" Cyrus, Mr. Edward, and Mrs. Pauline Perkins. Others, including seamstresses Mrs. Susie Saunders, Mrs. Gaston, and Mrs. Edward

Wood, made clothing for the local ladies to wear on special occasions. Ed and Mamie Jones, Joe and Lillian Thomas, and Arthur Battle were among those who managed a local hotel. Dry cleaning, pressing, and tailoring were the forte of J. C. Ware, Ed Reed, Arthur Battle, Arthur Spigner, William Hill, Oscar Wheeler, and Pete Trumbell over the years. There was a tearoom, run by Mrs. Penny Bowers.

Before refrigerators, Mrs. Stanley's account continued, people bought ice from Oscar W. Hazlett's wagon. Charles McCoy's hot barbecue cart was a popular fixture on the weekends for many years. Three generations enjoyed the fresh vegetables of Alex Adams, known as "the vegetable man." Early neighborhood grocers were Fred Prince, Amos Hughes, Roy Franklin, James Griffin, Miss Estelle Battle, Paul Lee, Phil Davis, and Ollie Lincoln.

The black community in Port Huron had its social set, too: The oldest black social club, established in 1928, was the 400 Club. Then came the Topper Club, the Cosmopolitan Club, and the Workingman's Club. All these clubs were interested in bringing cultural involvement to the community and doing work with young people.

Among the healers was Dr. Charles Williams, the first residential black doctor in Port Huron, and Dr. Orr, the first black dentist. When it was time to give birth, "Mama" Lizzie Hill, Annie Bates, and Mrs. Edward Wood, Sr. were the midwives to call. Those who preferred herb healing visited "Mama" Lizzie Hill and "Mother" Emma Johnson and Reverend Charles Thompson.

For entertainment, there were pool rooms (although they were frowned upon), one of which was run by a Reverend L. L. Strickland. But the most popular place in town, the only place to hang out and drink and listen to music, was the Red Shingle, owned by the Harvey family since 1934.

"It was originally located in the downtown area, on a street called Grand River," says the current owner, Spurgeon Harvey, a large, outgoing man who in the late 1970s was the first black man to be elected to the local board of commissioners. "Soldiers would come through, black and white prostitutes, and jazz musicians too. Elger Harvey, my uncle, was the focal point. It is a bar that has a lot of black history." During World War II, the Shingle, as it is locally called, became pretty well known overseas, in large part because of soldiers who would talk about it; many of its visitors said they learned about it from the servicemen they met in the war.

But for many in the black community of Port Huron, there wasn't really much to do, nothing truly stimulating for entertainment except drinking, screwing, and gossiping—the usual pastimes in any small community when there aren't all that many jobs, and brutal winters besides. The more enterprising of that bunch sold food and drinks, or rented rooms in their houses, or had gambling parties with cards and craps, and some of the women turned tricks.

It was this portion of the black community that Terry McMillan rather transparently "fictionalized" in *Mama*. Or put another way, she immortalized it. The names of most of the people and places are clearly recognizable to all those who live there, and to some who don't: She gives the town the name of Point Haven, describing it as being in "the thumb of Michigan." She mentions Lake Huron, the St. Clair River, Sarnia, Ontario, South Park, the black section, the street names, and the auto factories (Ford, General Motors, Chrysler).

In the book, Terry's scorching description of the demographics in both the black and white communities was not exactly one that the local chamber of commerce would have written, but it got the message across: "Coming from Detroit, you reached South Park first, and the first impression people got was that this place looked like a ghost town. It was. Full of black ghosts . . . with no place to go besides the Shingle."

Later, she noted that "Those on welfare looked for opportunities in all employable cracks and crevices but once they found jobs, many of them realized that their welfare checks were steadier and went a lot further. So a lot of them stopped looking altogether and spent their afternoons watching soap operas and gossiping." Then there was the area "where middle-class white folks who thought they were upper class lived. The only black folks you ever saw up there were the ones who cleaned house, raked leaves, or picked up trash."

Terry's take on the sociology of that part of the town was that "Drinking was the single most reliable source of entertainment for a lot of people in Point Haven. Alcohol was a genuine elixir, granting instant relief from the mundane existence that each and every one of them led. No one was the least bit curious about anything that went on outside Point Haven. Most of the black men couldn't find jobs, and as a result, they had so much spare time on their hands that when they were stone-cold broke, bored with themselves, or pissed off about everything because life turned out to be such a disappointment, their dissatisfaction would burst open and their rage would explode. This was what usually passed for masculinity, and it was often their wives or girlfriends or whores who felt the fallout."

One name she didn't change in the book was that of the Red Shingle. "Folks hung out at the Red Shingle," she wrote, "because it was the only place blacks were welcome."

On July 28, 1930, Felix Washington, a twenty-one-year-old Alabama native who worked as a foundryman, married Mary Bell Noble, an eighteen-year-old North Carolina girl. Despite— or because of—the fact that each was an only child, they began their family of six children: three boys, LaVern, Rudolph, and Felix, Jr.; and three girls, Jean, Sylvia, and Madeline Katherine. Madeline, who would be Terry's mother, was born in Port Huron on December 15, 1933.

As her brother LaVern later stated in an interview with the local newspaper, Madeline "was what in my day was called a tomboy. She'd put on a pair of boxing gloves and if you weren't careful, she'd body slam you."

Tomboy or not, in the winter of 1950 while Harry S. Truman was president, at the age of seventeen, Madeline became pregnant. It might have been the music: Nat "King" Cole was warbling "Mona Lisa" out of every radio, which in black Port Huron was usually tuned to Detroit radio station WJLB. Sarah Vaughan, Billie Holiday, Frank Sinatra, and the debonair bass-baritone of the excruciatingly handsome Billy Eckstine could also, in certain situations, melt a person into doing something naughty. Or it could have been those pointy new uplift bras that the girls were wearing under their sweaters. Whatever it was, on June 9 of the next year, five months pregnant and having only finished the eleventh grade in high school, Madeline married twenty-one-year-old Edward Lewis McMillan, known locally as Crook. Crook was one of the youngest of the five boys in the McMillan family. Headed by William McMillan and Gustava Manley McMillan, this family was allegedly one of Port Huron's more "hell-raising" families, with nine kids altogether (Edward had four brothers and four sisters).

Madeline's baby, a girl, was born on October 18, 1951. It was a mild Thursday, and Port Huron, black and white, was getting ready for Halloween: downtown at Kresge's ("open Friday night until 9:00"), Halloween costumes ("children's ready-made outfits in loud colors") were $1.79 and $2.98. Gumdrops were twenty-five cents a pound, Hershey or Nestle Miniature Bars were forty cents a pound.

For entertainment, that day's *Port Huron Times-Herald* announced that at the Desmond Theatre, *The Highwayman* ("Starts TODAY") starring Charles Coburn opened. *David & Bathsheba* was about to open ("Coming Sun.").

Other ads in the newspaper offered such items as a colonial maple five-piece dinette set for $79.95 "on easy terms" at Economy Furniture Co. on Military Street. For women, black suede pumps were $13.95 at Ballentine's, and nylon bras were seventy-seven cents at Penny's.

Local grocery shoppers could make their lists from the paper's IGA supermarket ad, which trumpeted Del Monte Pumpkin (large 2½ size cans) at two for thirty-five cents. A pound of Blue Bonnet Margarine was twenty-nine cents, of Hills Bros. Coffee seventy-nine cents, of ground beef sixty-three cents, and of ham fifty-three cents.

Although probably not in any condition to read that day's newspaper, young Madeline, two months shy of her eighteenth birthday, now had one more mouth to feed. She named her firstborn daughter Terry Lynn McMillan. Terry would be the first of five children.

Was it possible that a couple of the important literary events—or better said, events in the world of words—of that year would have a karmic effect on the newborn Terry? In July, three months before Terry's birth, Jerome David (J. D.) Salinger's *Catcher in the Rye* had been published. *Catcher in the Rye* was a revolutionary novel: Its teenage hero and narrator is Holden Caulfield, a rebellious, confused prep school dropout. Restlessly roaming around New York City, Holden learns to deal with both his own weaknesses and the hypocrisy of adults. Salinger's book, which accurately captured the everyday language, gestures, and pissed-off attitude of some young adults, would become a classic.

The second event occurred exactly two weeks after Terry's

birth: on November 1, 1951, the first issue of *Jet*, a weekly newsmagazine covering black America, appeared on the newsstands. The magazine, the first of its kind, was published by a remarkable black man, John H. Johnson, publisher of the six-year-old *Ebony* magazine. Now, black Americans would have yet another source, published by black Americans, which regularly reported on the lives and positive achievements of black celebrities, politicians, entertainers, and others. And decades later, both *Jet* and *Ebony* magazines would report on Terry's achievements as an author and screenwriter.

Or could it have been the stars? Terry was born under the astrological sign of Libra, the seventh sign of the zodiac, a cardinal air sign. It is a positive, masculine sign, ruled by the planet Venus, and takes its name from the Latin word for pound weight, or scales, which are its symbol. The key phrase of Libra is "I Balance." The entrance of the sun into Libra begins a new season, which is fall.

Astrologists say that many people born under Libra have strong artistic tendencies and a refined sense of style. That they tend to be socially inclined and charming, but they may have a need to be liked that makes them too compliant to others' wishes. That they are able to see all sides of an argument, but as their mental scales sway back and forth, they may never find balance and become fickle and indecisive. Sociable, seductive, and attractive, the cultural awareness and talkative nature of Librans help them shine in the social situations they so enjoy. But because of their social nature, they can be vain or overly dependent on the approval of others, and are happiest when they're in a relationship; yet, they can become lazy and apathetic if bored. Words used to describe Librans include *romantic, enthusiastic, changeable, artistic, persuasive, self-protective, strong, aggressive, argumentative, sensual,* and *sensitive.*

Perhaps it could have been the numbers—or more accurately, the numerology. Those who believe in the ancient practice of numerology—which is the use of numbers to analyze character and foretell the future—believe that the universe is governed by numerical laws and that each number has special powers and qualities. In numerology, one's name and date of birth gives important clues to one's character. With the birth date, for example, each number in the person's birth date is "reduced" to one digit. In the most simple interpretation, the numbers are added together, and the separate figures in the total are combined to arrive at a number from one to nine. This number is said to be the life path or destiny number. Terry's life path number is eight. Those whose life path number is eight are said to be self-confident, ambitious, stubborn, and rigid, and concerned with accomplishment and accumulation of money and material possessions (and willing to work hard to get them).

But literary karma, stars, and numbers were only metaphysical factors in Terry's personality. Closer to earth, and far more tangible, there was Madeline.

Terry's mother Madeline was, well, a trip. She was funny, quick-witted, and had a ready supply of one-line jokes that kept people in stitches; few people who talked to her could ever forget the conversation. Madeline was a proud, dignified, spunky, fearless lady. If there was anything she was afraid of, she wouldn't show it: Her motto was "Feel the fear and do it anyway!" She welcomed challenges, and knew how to overcome obstacles.

Madeline's strong personality could be overwhelming to people who did not understand her, and sometimes her way of doing things rubbed people the wrong way. But she cared about people, and earned a reputation for being forthright and honest. As a friend, she was supportive and sympathetic, though she may not have always said what her friends wanted to hear.

Madeline referred to herself as a "red-hot motor scooter," and would explain that when God made her, He threw away the mold. Fully aware of all her senses, Madeline had needs, she had desires, she had ideas, she had advice, and she was not ashamed of any of them.

If economics had not dictated that Madeline raise five children in a small town, she most certainly would have been something else—perhaps, as her daughter Rosalyn later wrote, a standup comedian. But less than thirteen months after Terry's birth, Edwin was born, on November 10, 1952; eleven months later, on October 14, 1953, Rosalyn was born; Crystal was born November 2, 1955; and ten months after that, on September 11, 1956, Vicki was born.

In the pages of *Mama,* Terry recycles this history, and more. In the book, the first initial of Mildred's name was the first initial of Madeline's name. Her other characters' nicknames weren't too far away from their real-life counterparts, either: Mildred's husband was named Crook, which was the real-life nickname of Edward McMillan, Terry's father. The character Money, Mildred's only son, was named after Terry's brother Edwin, whose real-life nickname was Money.

The character Mildred's childbearing pattern was similar to Madeline's: She had Freda (Terry) when she was seventeen, "and the other kids had fallen out every nine or ten months after that, with the exception of one year between Freda and Money."

There are, of course, storylines in *Mama* that only the family would know. For example, early in the book, Terry mentions that Crook, Mildred's husband, didn't believe that Freda, the oldest daughter (this would be Terry's fictional counterpart), was his natural child. He suspected that Freda was the child of one Percy Russell. However, there is no evidence of that in the Port Huron public records.

Madeline was not one to sit around and complain. She just became a red-hot motor scooter of a mother, too, treating motherhood as a career. Her children were fascinated and inspired by her attitude, her personality, her motivation, and the lessons she taught them.

First, even though Madeline had never been out of Port Huron, she taught her children that there was a big world outside of Port Huron. As Terry said later, "She made us see that the world was not so small. She used to tell us to see everything, even if you do come back home."

Second, she taught them, mostly by example, that although they might be living in a poor neighborhood, there was no need to *act* poor. Even if you didn't *have,* you could have high standards. So Madeline dressed her children in nice clothes; Terry and her sisters wore Jonathan Logan dresses, even when Madeline could hardly afford them.

Third, in a practical way, she encouraged her children to be independent. She gave them solid advice, like "Always have a thick skin—people are going to talk about you if you do and talk about you if you don't," and "If you don't have an opinion about something, get one, because you'll need it." She taught them all to sew. She wanted her girls to grow up to be educated, strong, smart, independent, and reliable. "I don't want you growing up and having to depend on no man for everything," she cautioned them.

It could have been that Madeline's outlook was genetically passed on to Terry. Maybe Terry noticed the boredom settling over other folks' lives, and took that as a kind of warning. It could have been that Terry was what people call "an old soul." Or she could have just been a person who gets bored easily. But whatever it was, Terry did not like Port Huron; it did not feel interesting or stimulating enough to put down roots and spend a life there. "I didn't like where I grew up," she has said. "It could be a dreadful place. It's really pretty, but it was not very stimulating. There was nothing to do; nobody's life was eventful." So it was fortuitous that at least in the McMillan household, no one was ridiculed for being dissatisfied with the status quo or dreaming of being Elsewhere. Although they lived in a small town, there was no need to act as if that was all there was.

The McMillan family lived downstairs at 3119 Moak Street, in the South Park section of Port Huron. Covered in an asphalt-based exterior siding material known as Insul-Brick, 3119 was a big, rambling, ugly two-story house with a couple of porches protruding from it. It sat in the middle of a grassy, two-acre corner plot right next to the tracks of the Port Huron & Detroit Railway (a private railroad), surrounded by trees, with no pavement. At least one other family lived in the house. In *Mama,* Terry describes the house at Moak as being on Thirty-second Street, right at the railroad crossing, "sitting in the middle of two acres of land, with a rolling front yard so long and so wide, most of the other inhabitants had used a riding lawn mower to cut the grass. There were pear trees, apple trees, a plum tree, and blackberry bushes in the woods that stood at the edge of the backyard."

Despite Madeline's upbeat attitude, life wasn't all that jolly at 3119 Moak Street. Edward, who was a sanitation worker, was also a diabetic and an alcoholic, and these illnesses prevented him from having a perfect attendance record at work. Frustrated and angry, he would beat Madeline regularly. "My mother didn't just get beat up," Terry said. "She fought back. A lot of times she kicked my father's ass." And the five kids often "would jump on him to break it up." But Terry was critical of her mother for putting up with that kind of treatment.

Madeline worked wherever she could. Sometimes she got work in the local factories, such as the automobile factory or the pickle factory; other times she cleaned people's homes. When things were really bad, she went on welfare between factory jobs. The McMillan kids were forced to be responsible at an early age: They raked leaves, baby-sat, and worked in clothing stores to help make ends meet. Terry took care of her brother and sisters, too, cooking, washing their hair, and making sure they did their homework. "When we grew up poor, we weren't sitting around being depressed. If all you have is pork and beans and hot dogs, you add a little catsup and scoop it up," Terry said.

Like a lot of their neighbors, the McMillans struggled. They moved several times, and there were some tough Michigan winters when they went without a phone, heat, or electricity. "There were a couple winter nights when I remember my teeth chattering," Terry said. "But I don't remember ever feeling poor. I hate that word. We never went hungry."

In spite of the tension at home, Madeline expected her children to do well. "You will go to college," she told Terry, "and you're not going with a baby. You keep your little legs closed and keep your mind on your books."

"When we got good grades, it was a reflection on her," Terry said. "Even though she only got up to eleventh grade, that was her way of saying, 'I'm doing something right.' We didn't have time to fail. She didn't give us that space. For an uneducated woman, she's probably one of the smartest women I'll ever meet in my life. And I'm grateful to her for what she gave me. She taught me how to think, that's what she did. And to let people know what you think."

To supplement Madeline's good old-fashioned home training, Terry's formal education began when she was five years old, when she entered kindergarten at the Cleveland Elementary School on Vanness Street in Port Huron's South Park section.

It was an extremely poor, underprivileged area, with a high unemployment rate. Built in 1923, the school wasn't far from the McMillan home on Moak and Thirty-second. The school held six grades, with thirty to thirty-five children per classroom.

Marguerite Stanley remembers, "The school system wasn't segregated. Everybody went to the same school. You just went to school in your district."

Terry's kindergarten teacher was Mary Goschnik, who was twenty-eight years old at the time. In the kindergarten class photo, a smiling little Terry is wearing black and white oxford shoes with white socks.

"She was a fine little student," remembers Mary Goschnik. "I remember she was always real clean. I had one student who was so dirty I had to send her home to take a bath—made her mother mad! I would call Terry an A-minus student. She was always there, almost never absent. She had an outgoing personality. She was a happy person. All the kids around the neighborhood were friends.

"At that time we didn't do a whole lot—we did preparation for first grade. They did not have workbooks. I had a nice playhouse. I did a lot of stuff with them. We had a lot of field trips—there was a florist that lived not too far away, and we probably walked to his place. We visited the firemen because we had a fire station nearby.

"I've got her book *Mama* on my coffee table right now, and when I read it I know exactly who she's talking about and I could pick out each one. Because I went to each one of the children's homes one year at Christmas—teachers don't do much of that anymore—just to see where they were from and get a better understanding of them."

By the time Terry was in kindergarten, it was the early 1960s. John F. Kennedy had begun his term as president in January 1961, and the civil rights movement, under the leadership of Dr. Martin Luther King, Jr., was growing. It was the height of the Cold War, the Berlin Wall had gone up in 1961, and in 1962 came the Cuban missile crisis.

Inevitably, the marriage between Madeline and Edward McMillan ended in divorce in May of 1963. Madeline was the plaintiff; according to the divorce judgment, she brought the action on the grounds of "extreme and repeated cruelties." Madeline was awarded custody of the children: Terry was eleven, Edwin ten, Rosalyn nine, Crystal seven, and Vicki six. They were still living in South Park, but had moved to 2203 Twenty-fifth Street, a mostly unpaved avenue a couple of blocks south of the railroad tracks.

And the sixties rolled along. Although 1963 was the centennial anniversary of the Emancipation Proclamation, blacks were still the victims of racial prejudice. They had migrated from southern states like Mississippi, Georgia, and Alabama, to northern industrial cities such as Detroit in search of jobs and a better way of non-cotton-picking life. Still, conditions were tough for most, and in August 1963, 200,000 blacks and concerned whites traveled to Washington, D.C., to demonstrate for equal rights. In November 1963, President Kennedy was assassinated, and his civil rights bill was passed under his successor, Lyndon Johnson, in 1964. But blacks in the slums of the north remained discontented; frustrations over living conditions and job opportunities continued, reaching a peak during the devastating Watts riots of 1965 in Los Angeles.

Young blacks were concerned about the question of violence versus nonviolence, and whether to unite with whites or segregate from them. The Black Power movement was growing, and the Black Panthers—an organization whose aim was to protect blacks from police harassment while staying within the law—were making headlines. In 1964 the U.S. intervened in Vietnam, and many students got involved in the black civil rights movement and protests against Vietnam. On February 21, 1965, the black community was stunned to hear the news that black Muslim leader Malcolm X had been assassinated. But in Port Huron, not many in the black community even knew who he was. As Terry described her fictional-but-really-Port-Huron town in *Mama,* "Most folks had never heard of Malcolm X and only a few had some idea who Martin Luther King was. They lived as if they were sleepwalking or waiting around for something else to happen." There was a local chapter of the NAACP in Port Huron and they kept an eye on things, but there were no noteworthy racial incidents in the town.

The sixties was also a decade when young people created their own culture, spending their money and free time on clothes and music. Writers, poets, and some jazz musicians, influenced by the beat culture of the fifties, read or performed their works wearing handmade sandals, black turtlenecks, black berets, and tight black pants. Pop music charts were taken over by young artists, who made music for their contemporaries: The British invasion, featuring the Beatles, the Who, and the Rolling Stones, was well under way.

But so was Motown. An hour south of Port Huron, Berry Gordy was cranking out hits that combined soul rhythms with smooth melodies. The Supremes, Mary Wells, the Temptations, the Four Tops, Smokey Robinson, Marvin Gaye, and many others racked up hit after hit after hit, and black pop flooded the country. At the other end of the black music spectrum, harder, nastier, more raw, there was James Brown, the Godfather of Soul, inventor of funk. And R & B artists such as Otis Redding, Wilson Pickett, and Aretha Franklin. In the jazz world, modern musicians like Miles Davis and John Coltrane were at the peak of their careers. There was music—good music—for every mood.

During the sixties, many young blacks stopped using chemicals to straighten their natural curls. The result was the Afro: Grown as long as possible and neatly shaped, it was a display of black pride that caught on in a big way. Other young blacks were influenced by the black berets and military style of the Black Panthers, or the flamboyant dress adopted by other black radicals and black musicians: caftans, unisex dashikis, headbands, beads, fringes, and tassels on everything, and exotic accessories imported from exotic countries like Morocco and Turkey.

And there was the psychedelic explosion going on on the West Coast, in the San Francisco Bay Area which would one day become Terry's home, where marijuana and LSD were being experimented with, enjoyed, and advocated by a small circle of hippies, whose attitude, just like the beatniks, was Outrageous behavior is okay, daddy-o. Get hip. Do your own thing. Feel groovy.

But in South Park, things were pretty much unchanged. National events made headlines and earned articles in the *Port Huron Times-Herald,* but not too much happened locally as a result. Everyday living was hard enough, with the two main priorities being making a living and making love.

Now a single, struggling woman, Madeline McMillan had taken up with a younger man, who at thirteen years Madeline's junior was a man closer to Terry's age than her own. His name was Alvin Tillman, a Mississippi-born laborer also known as Nicky.

So on October 8, 1967, four and a half years after her divorce from Edward McMillan, Madeline, then thirty-three, married Alvin Tillman. At the time, the family was living a few streets over from the big house on Moak, at 3109 Thirtieth Street. Young Terry was fifteen years old; Alvin was only five years older than she was.

There is a point in the book *Mama* that may draw upon the Alvin/Madeline marriage: Mildred, having just been dumped by one of her lovers, latches onto Rufus, a dependable friend of the family who, although he didn't like to bathe all that much, "treats me nice and keeps some money in his pocket at all times." Against the protests of her children—especially Freda—Mildred decides to marry him.

Two pages later, when Mildred tells Rufus she wants a divorce, Rufus pulls a knife on her and Freda comes to her defense, screaming "Let go of my mama, you son-of-a-bitch!" and with superhuman strength, the strength of the driven, Freda grabs him, tosses him, and in the struggle gains control of the knife and holds it to *his* throat.

Many times in interviews Terry has recounted such an incident between herself and her stepfather, saying that when she was about fourteen, she broke up a fight between her mother and her stepfather by grabbing his knife and putting it to his throat, demanding, "How's it feel now?"

"Without realizing it, I turned into one of those people who can turn cars over to save people," she told Michael Shelden, a reporter for the *Daily Telegraph,* a national British newspaper. "I lifted him up by the shirt, and threw him. The knife fell from his hand, and I grabbed it. I took that knife, and I pushed that point into his neck and said: 'Now, how does that feel?' " In an exaggerated, weepy voice, she imitates her mother saying: " 'Terry, put the knife down. You don't know what you're doing. It's scaring me.' I told him, 'You know what? You touch my mother again, and I will slit your throat.' And he knew— he knew—that if he said the wrong thing, I would slit his throat. And I would have."

In 1968, the phrase "black is beautiful" was first coined. At the Olympics in Mexico, two medal-winning black American athletes refused to salute the flag during the national anthem, giving the clenched-fist Black Power salute instead. But there was no empowerment in the Tillman marriage.

On November 18, 1968, thirteen months after the marriage, Alvin moved out, or was thrown out by Madeline. Madeline filed a complaint for divorce through William H.

Ryan, Esq., the same lawyer who had represented her in *Mc-Millan v. McMillan*. A restraining order—resulting from Madeline's petition stating that "defendant has struck and hit the plaintiff, and has broken windows in the home of the plaintiff, and the plaintiff is apprehensive for her own safety and the well-being of her children"—was served on Tillman on January 17, 1969. On January 20, a summons for divorce was served on him, with a complaint alleging that "during the marriage defendant has been guilty of acts of extreme and repeated cruelties."

On March 17, a judgment of divorce was granted, and Madeline was once again a single mama. That was also the year that Edward McMillan died, succumbing to the double pathologies of alcoholism and diabetes.

Terry was seventeen years old that year and a student at Port Huron High School. One of her best subjects was typing: She was fast, and she was good. At the time, Terry and her girlfriends Cynthia Morgan and Bernadine Harvey were like the Three Musketeers. Bernadine's mom was a seamstress, and they shared clothes such as tent dresses (they hardly ever wore pants). After school and on weekends, they went to ball games, the Cleveland School recreation center, and of course had sleepovers at one another's houses. But the most fun of all was going to dances at places called the Sundown and the Hut, where they did the Hully Gully, the Monkey, the Mashed Potatoes, the Jerk, the Social, and the Bop to the music of either live bands; Motown favorites; make-you-sweat tunes like James Brown's "Papa's Got a Brand New Bag," "I Got You," or "Cold Sweat;" or cool grooves like Ramsey Lewis's "The In Crowd." The music was so good that if there wasn't a guy to dance with, two girls would.

"Terry was the ugly duckling of the family," remembers one neighbor. "Her sisters were considered 'strapped.' Rosalyn and the rest of them had big legs, big ass, big hips. Maybe that was why Terry was kinda hostile—she couldn't get any action!"

All the McMillan kids were still doing what they could to help their mother make ends meet. When Terry was sixteen years old and a sophomore in high school, she got her first paying job. For $1.25 an hour, she was a student page in the St. Clair County Public Library in downtown Port Huron. Her responsibility was to reshelve books that had been returned.

The St. Clair County Public Library is a two-story, beige brick structure in the downtown Port Huron area. It sits a block away from the St. Clair River and across the street from the county courthouse and other municipal buildings.

Although Terry was a good reader who enjoyed reading, up to that point, she has said, her only exposure to books had been the required reading for school. All the authors of those books happened to be white males—Ralph Waldo Emerson, William Faulkner, Nathaniel Hawthorne, Ernest Hemingway, Thomas Mann, Henry Thoreau—which she had dutifully read but considered boring. In fact, Terry assumed that *all* authors were white.

The only book in the McMillan home was a rarely used Bible, and neither Madeline, Edward, nor Alvin had read to the children. Although there were no books in the house, there was television, and to relieve her young boredom, Terry zoned out on programs like *Hawaii 5-0*, the action police series filmed in Hawaii, and *Adventures in Paradise*, an adventure series based loosely on the fiction of James Michener about the skipper of a small schooner in the South Pacific.

But on the shelves of the library, Terry discovered another place to zone out. She was introduced to the world of books and to reading for pleasure. There were so many other books, she discovered, besides those boring classics she had to read in school. Sitting on the floor of the library's travel section, she would read and fantasize. Now, she had another way, besides television, of escaping the stifling boundaries of Port Huron.

One of the books that moved Terry was a biography of Louisa May Alcott, who in 1868 wrote *Little Women*, the autobiographical novel of her childhood which became a classic. Here was a young girl that Terry could identify with. Louisa, like Terry, had to help support her family at a young age, and Terry related to her situation—after all, that's why she was working at the library. "I was excited because I had not really read about poor white folks before," Terry wrote later. During Louisa May Alcott's childhood, her family lived in Boston near the docks. Young Louisa wrote in her journal about the poverty of her family, the hunger, the overcrowding of too many people in one "dilapidated red farmhouse," of having bread and water for breakfast, bread and water and a vegetable for lunch, and bread and water and fruit for supper. But venturing out of her own small, depressing environment, Louisa was impressed by the contrast between the poor neighborhoods and the prosperous ones. This small realization—that there was another way of living, other places to be lived in, than where she lived—gave her something to aspire to.

Surely this struck more than one chord in Terry. She herself lived in Port Huron, always within shouting distance of the railroad tracks. All the houses she had ever lived in were within the sound of the freight trains carrying coal and fly ash for the power company, rumbling from Port Huron to Marine City thirty miles south. The houses in South Park were made of wood, many in disrepair, and most of the streets were unpaved. Yet the affluent neighborhoods, like the one in which the St. Clair County Public Library was located, were clean and bright, with sidewalks. There was another way of living, other places to be lived in, than where she lived. Louisa and Terry had a few things in common, yes they had.

Terry never acted poor, though. Just because she lived in a poor community, she did not claim and own poverty like some of those she saw around her; she looked beyond it. Maybe she couldn't *have* certain things, but there was nothing stopping her from *looking* at them in magazines, newspapers, or on television. It cost not one cent to look at and observe things of good quality when she visited more affluent parts of town. Or when she shopped. Maybe she could only afford water, but that didn't stop her from looking at the soda bottles and visualizing! Terry maintained this trait all her life, always looking above and beyond. She created her own reality. This was one little girl who was not about to become a victim of her environment.

....

Terry's assumption that all authors were white was finally laid to rest at the library one day at work. Glancing at a book she was reshelving, in the spot where the author's picture usually was, she saw a photo of a black man. "Who in the world is this?" she wondered. Baldwin, that's who it was—James Baldwin, who by then had authored *Go Tell It on the Mountain, Notes of a Native Son, Giovanni's Room* (which most likely was not in *that* library!), *Another Country,* and *The Fire Next Time.* "Almost every book I used to put up was by a white author. So it never dawned on me that black people wrote books," she wrote. "I was not just naive, but had not yet acquired an ounce of black pride."

The following year, in 1969, Terry graduated from Port Huron High School. It was the school's one hundredth anniversary, having been established in 1869—five months after the Civil War ended—with the first class of four students. In the 1969 yearbook—*Student 1969*—there was mention of the newly organized Afro-American club, whose purpose was "to seek a better understanding of Negro history and literature. The members spend their Wednesday evenings at the local YMCA discussing the past and present conditions of the Negro in America. The club also held dances in which the proceeds were used to finance trips and materials."

The yearbook shows that all the teachers were white except Mr. Manis Johnson, Industrial Education and Ms. Willa McDowell, Home Economics. Of the thirty-three student council members, three were black: Morris Hall, Janice Stanley, and Carol Falk.

In her yearbook photo, Terry is flashing a huge smile—could it have been delight in some hidden, intuitive, mysterious knowledge that there was some adventure up ahead? Or was it that she was on the way toward losing the bet she'd made with her girlfriends to see who would lose their virginity first? (According to one high-school report, Terry did, giving it up at eighteen to some guy nicknamed "Bubbles," said to be her boyfriend in her last year of high school.)

Even then, Terry favored big earrings: In the photo, Terry wears big dangly earrings, the biggest of all the girls in the book—and wore her straightened hair in a short page-boy style, almost like a 1920s flapper.

Also in the yearbook, there is a more significant photo: of Terry and her classmates in the Business Education department's Office Practice class. "To advance the accuracy of the student as quickly as possible" was the teacher's main objective. Terry was one of the best typists in the class . . . and a good thing, too. Typing would become her meal ticket.

2

Leaving the Place of Oppression

Talent is very common. But few people have the will, the energy, and the drive to get over.

—Ishmael Reed, one of Terry's college professors

Terry graduated from Port Huron High School with a passport to the future: She had a skill—typing and shorthand—and she knew how to use it.

Still, she could see no future for herself in Port Huron. Neither factory work nor domestic work held any interest for her, and she certainly did not possess the temperament for either. Besides, for years she'd gotten an up close and personal look at what those kinds of work could do to a person, including her mother and other folks she knew around town. She couldn't sing or play an instrument, so a trip to Detroit to park herself before Berry Gordy at Motown Records wasn't an option, either. But her burning desire to venture beyond her boundaries led her to make a huge leap: Sometime between June and October of 1969, she simply split. Put Port Huron behind her.

Some accounts report that she turned down a college scholarship.

Terry's actual departure from Port Huron is not documented, and may or may not have taken place the way the character Freda's departure from Point Haven did in *Mama*. In the book, well tired of Point Haven, Freda decides to get out of town by writing her cousin Phyllis in Los Angeles to ask if she can come out there and stay with her until she can get a job, and then go to college. "When I do finish college, I'ma do something that's gon' make me rich, maybe even famous," Freda promises her mama. With her mother's blessing, Freda saves her money from her job as a part-time keypunch operator at the phone company, and flies to Los Angeles the August after she graduates from high school and soon finds a job as a secretary.

The real Terry most likely took her savings, bought a one-way plane or bus ticket, packed her little undies and a few pairs of big earrings, and took the flight, or two-day bus ride, west to California and college. She liked the idea of helping people, and there was a partially formed idea in her mind of perhaps enrolling in college and studying to be a social worker.

Once Terry made the decision to leave the place that her soul was telling her to escape from, her life became magical. Taking that leap into the unknown was exactly the act of faith that made her life begin to happen. She didn't know it at the time, of course—we live our lives forward, but appreciate them backward—but following her instincts was the right step to take. And from that moment, things—seen and unseen—began to happen that both led her and aided her on her journey to becoming a writer. She would encounter and be affected by kindred spirits. Writers, both living and dead, famous and not-yet famous, in person and on pages . . . she would be touched by a whole universe of them. But right now, she was just a poor black girl from Michigan, going to see what she could see.

When Terry left Port Huron in 1969, she was seventeen years old. Once she arrived in Los Angeles, she found mountains, palm trees, perpetual warm weather, no winters, creative people—and work as a secretary. For a while, typewriters, stiff white bond paper, crinkly black carbon paper, round erasers with brushes on the ends, and spools of inked ribbon were her constant companions. Soon—although it is not clear exactly when or how—Terry's mother and the kids followed, joining her in California.

In *Mama,* after Freda returns to Point Haven for a visit, her eye is even more critical of the place: "Most of the girls she had gone to high school with were living in the projects with one or two babies, and they were big and fat and quite a few of them needed dental work. The guys seemed to spend all of their waking hours in front of the pool hall, drinking wine or nodding over cigarettes . . . It was this town. This termite of a place which would sooner or later eat away her mama and the girls too." So Freda convinces her mama to move to Los Angeles with two of her sisters (the remaining one has gotten married, and the son, Crook, is in jail, having succumbed to the dangers of the street). In reality, this may or may not have been how the McMillan clan got to Los Angeles.

One day, Terry got her hands on the catalog of Los Angeles City College, a public community college established in 1929.

With a campus sprawling over forty acres, it was the original site of UCLA; during the 1930s, the original buildings—torn down by the time Terry arrived—were used as a college campus movie backdrop. As a public community college, tuition was free for residents, so Terry may have decided to wait the required one year and establish Los Angeles residency, thereby becoming eligible for free tuition, rather than paying the $13 per credit that nonresidents were charged. Anyway, her typing and shorthand skills were her meal ticket, and there were always, always secretarial jobs available.

As she later wrote, what caught her eye in that LACC catalog was a class called "Afro-American Literature." Even though she wondered if there were enough black writers to devote a whole course to, she enrolled, eager to find out about this new genre.

And so began Terry's first surge of black pride, her first lessons in black culture, and her immersion in black history. Through the class textbook, *Dark Symphony: Negro Literature in America,* and authors like Countee Cullen, Ralph Ellison, Langston Hughes, Zora Neale Hurston, Ann Petry, Jean Toomer, Richard Wright, and her old buddy James Baldwin, she discovered a whole new world. She wrote, "I accumulated and gained a totally new insight about, and perception of, our lives as black people, as if I had been an outsider and was finally let in. To discover that our lives held as much significance and importance as our white counterparts was more than gratifying, it was exhilarating."

Although those writers made a huge impact on Terry, she

was still only reading—not writing. Besides, she was in love for the first time, according to her.

But in 1971, when she was twenty years old, her man, whoever he was, broke her heart. Wounded, hurting, broken, she could only release her feelings in one way: on paper. Not in a letter, not in a journal entry, but in a poem. Terry wrote a poem about her heartbreak.

Later, she would explain, "I did not sit down and say, 'I'm going to write a poem about this.' It was more like magic. I didn't even know I was writing a poem until I had written it. Afterward, I felt lighter, as if something had happened to lessen the pain."

When a friend of hers who had just launched a black literary magazine at the college saw it on her kitchen table, he read it. She was embarrassed and shocked—not that he read it, but when he said he liked it, and even more when he asked if he could publish it in the magazine. In the midst of tragedy, a star was born. Terry's magic had begun. The karma was rolling: That poem, which she wrote because of something personal that had happened to her, was Terry's first published piece.

What an ego boost to see one's name in print! But more important than that, the dam had burst. Poems flowed out of Terry like water, and many of them appeared in the college publications. Her poems were sassy, sharp, and covered many topics, whatever came to her mind, but were mostly her observations and feelings as a young black woman searching for her place in the world. They were "short poems, smart-ass and flippant and kind of pop cultural," noted Clyde Taylor, a black

UCLA professor who knew her. But as ego boosting as it was to see her name in print, Terry knew that most writers were starving—even though she knew no writers. And if it was that bad for writers, forget poets. Terry also knew that people who wrote *poems* were starving even more: No poet could make a living off writing poetry. Terry couldn't envision herself as a starving *anything,* and she was not going there. "An idealistic twenty-two years old," as she referred to herself then, her goal was to make a decent living, and, being idealistic, she wanted to save the world or at least make a positive impact on people. Her conclusion was that becoming a social worker was the way to accomplish this, and Terry hopped onto the social worker track.

After completing two years at Los Angeles Community College, Terry transferred to the University of California at Berkeley (also known as UC Berkeley). Although she intended to major in sociology, in her heart she knew she wasn't really interested in the subject. Besides, the social work option had too many requirements that she felt she could not meet. Because writing was an easier thing for her—and because she was now writing short stories and the college newspaper had invited her to write editorials—Terry soon changed her major to journalism. But even that wasn't the perfect fit: Journalism, with its Who, What, When, Where, and Why format, was too structured for Terry's creative talent. Transforming her personal experiences and her questions about them into stories—that's what she enjoyed most.

Academics aside, it was the 1970s. And it was California. What a place for a young black woman to be! Black awareness was hot. Permissiveness was in. Black soul music and R & B were happening: The O'Jays, Curtis Mayfield, Sly & the Family Stone, Marvin Gaye, Donna Summer, Santana, War, Graham Central Station, Isaac Hayes, and Bob Marley all shared space on the radio stations and in everyone's record collection. Discos, formerly meeting places for gays, blossomed into hot dance spots for all, in large part because of this black dance music.

Black faces began appearing more on stage and in movies, although mostly in "urban action" films in the roles of pimps, hustlers, drug dealers, and an occasional detective like the handsome Richard Roundtree as John Shaft. Veteran actors (Godfrey Cambridge, Scatman Crothers, Moses Gunn, Yaphet Kotto, Diana Sands) and new ones (Roscoe Lee Browne, Antonio Fargas, Sheila Frazier, Calvin Lockhart, Vonetta McGee, Melvin Van Peebles, Fred Williamson) were all familiar faces in such films. Such clichéd use of black talent in these movies came to be known as "blaxploitation," and the movies were given the nickname "blaxploitation films."

From 1971 to 1973, such movies were everywhere. The adventures of sexy New York City private detective John Shaft kept female eyes glued to the screen during the 1971 movie *Shaft*, as well as its 1972 sequel, *Shaft's Big Score*. That year also brought *Across 110th Street*, a violent tale of cops, the Mafia, and black criminals, set in Harlem; *Superfly,* directed by photographer Gordon Parks, which starred the yummily handsome Ron O'Neal as Priest, a New York dope pusher "trying to get over," as the Curtis Mayfield soundtrack explained; and six-foot-tall black beauty Pam Grier starred as a mercenary in *The Big Bird*

Cage. In 1973 there was a string of sequels such as *Shaft in Africa,* where the detective goes undercover to crush a modern slave trade, and *Superfly T.N.T.,* which brings Priest out of retirement to work on a foreign gun-running assignment. Scores and scripts were written by talented writers: Curtis Mayfield scored *Superfly,* and Isaac Hayes was the composer for the soundtrack of *Shaft,* for which he won the Grammy Award for Best Original Score and the Academy Award for Best Song in 1971. And Alex Haley, some three years before the publication of *Roots,* wrote the script for *Superfly T.N.T.* Further proof, perhaps, of the extremes to which writers sometimes must go to keep income rolling in?

And then there was the literary set. Black authors and poets of the 1970s whose work was widely read and whose names were much uttered in the black community included Maya Angelou, James Baldwin, Gwendolyn Brooks, Alice Childress, Ernest J. Gaines, Nikki Giovanni, June Jordan, John Oliver Killens, Toni Morrison, Ishmael Reed, Alice Walker, and John Edgar Wideman. Two new black magazines—*Black Enterprise,* a business magazine, and *Essence,* a women's lifestyle magazine—began publishing, providing an even larger forum for black authors. Several of these seventies authors would impact Terry's life in the next few years: Maya Angelou would endorse her writing, James Baldwin's work had already opened her eyes to the world of the black writer, John Oliver Killens was the founder of a writer's workshop that she would join, Ishmael Reed would become her teacher and mentor, Alice Walker would be someone whose recognition she would want, John Edgar Wideman would vacate a teaching position that Terry would later take, and her writing would eventually appear in *Essence* magazine.

"Write what you know." Every writer hears this advice, but for many, it's easy to dismiss. After all, we take our lives for granted, and it's hard to see any, well, literary merit in it. Even if we keep journals and can spin a yarn to our friends about a recent happening (or a series of them), for some people it is just not easy to stretch such a story into an interesting, captivating written piece.

Yet, looking at the classics, or any memorable stories, we realize that they are about basic things that touch all of us: love, jealousy, death, desire, the nature of existence. These yarns ask deep questions: Who are we? Why are we here? Where are we going? Writers are told that those are the very questions that can form the basis of a personal story about losing one's keys, or finding a job, or playing with one's child. Thus, our subject matter is always with us.

The trick—or the gift—is to understand and convey that our experience is not ours alone, but in a way, a metaphor for everyone else's. After all, we all go through childhood, adolescence, studenthood, adulthood, marriage, childbirth, parenthood, divorce, old age; we are brothers, sisters, mothers, fathers, friends, lovers. We are really more similar than different.

On a whim, one semester during the 1974–75 academic year, Terry enrolled in a class called Introduction to Fiction. The instructor was thirty-six-year-old-black poet, novelist, and essayist Ishmael Reed, who would in 1976 be a co-founder of the

Before Columbus Foundation, an organization devoted to re-defining American literature to reflect the country's diversity.

Ishmael Reed is a tall, friendly man about six feet tall, with a face that reflects his Cherokee Indian heritage. Thoroughly devoted to writers and the craft of writing, he has taught at Harvard, Yale, and Dartmouth; but his teaching career began at UC Berkeley in 1968. The year Terry took Reed's class, he had just returned from a three-year leave of absence.

"Out of that class came four other novelists: Mona Simpson, Fae Ng, Katie Trueblood, and Mitch Berman," says Reed. "I never had a class like that before, where that amount of talent came out of one class. That was a very lively class—they challenged each other.

"I do not impose my ideas of writing upon them. I try to get writers to discover their style, their voice. If their way of writing reminds me of somebody else's, I steer them to that person.

"I did not interfere with Terry's style. I think it was fully formed. She had something to say. She always had a good knack for a mien, she can always draw up different voices. She's not illustrating some kind of ideology, she's writing about people."

Reed gave Terry "mostly structural advice, on organization and questions of craft. She had all the stuff in her head. Most good writers have all the stuff in her head, they just have to structure it. So I helped her on form. What to leave out and what to leave in. That's a basic problem for most beginning writers. She became a cleaner writer in the workshop. I think she developed a lot in the workshop. Because they're very hard on each other, there's a lot of difficult criticism. What separated her from a lot of other people was her drive. She was focused about that."

To supplement Reed's coaching, Terry read, authors black and white. The satiric journalist and author Ring Lardner (1885–1933), was one of her favorites. "As soon as I read Ring Lardner," she later said, "his voice jumped off the page. What he was writing about was tragic, and I was cracking up. I realized that it was the same sort of thing I was trying to do." To Terry, Ring Lardner's message was " 'It's okay, Terry, to write the way that you talk.' Ring Lardner was the one who freed me up."

Other storytelling styles that Terry admired were those of Ann Petry (1909–97), who wrote *The Street,* a novel about a young black woman struggling to raise a son in the violence and poverty of 1940s Harlem, and Langston Hughes (1902–67), the Harlem Renaissance poet and author who wrote about his traveling adventures. Karmically speaking, Ann Petry's publisher, Houghton Mifflin, would be the publisher of Terry's first book.

Terry's first short story, "The End," impressed Ishmael Reed so much that he published it in 1976 in his literary magazine, *Yardbird Reader.* "It [*Yardbird Reader*] was something I founded around 1972," he explains. "We were devoted to publishing multicultural writers. I realized that students could write as well as anybody else, so I began to include students." Terry's story was one such student contribution.

Set in Detroit's lower east side, "The End" was a story about a young black man, Pobre Blackstone, who worked on the Ford assembly line and dreamed about the world coming to an end. Or is it really a dream?

"My work, my poetry, was not very lofty," Terry said once. "I have imitated Toni Morrison, John Wideman. But it's not honest for me. It's not my emotional reservoir. That's not what I'm filled up with."

An adult now, Terry had a small economic and social foothold: She was making a living, and she had friends that she did adult things with, like partying, traveling to local attractions like mountains and beaches, drinking, getting high, messing around with cocaine and alcohol. It was easy to meet guys, too. On Saturday nights, she would recall, folks called each other, asking "Where's the party?" Wherever it was, everyone would go to dance, talk, laugh, and flirt—with anyone who looked like a possibility. "Lots of times you spotted him or he spotted you, and he probably asked you to dance, and if you felt something special being in his arms or liked the tone of his voice or what he had to say after the song was over, then the night became much too short," she once wrote.

Terry herself had grown to about five feet seven inches, a little taller than average. As an adult, she had a loud, gravelly voice that could not be described as soft and demure. It was a more "street" tone of voice, reminiscent of a class bully containing the inflections that we use when we say "I'll kick yo' ass" or "Step outside" two of the common phrases that precede a street fight. Like most black women, she changed hairstyles frequently. She had clear skin and strong, attractive hands. But her most important physical attribute was her fingers—fast fingers, which when in contact with a typewriter keyboard, were her meal ticket.

At that age, like all young adults, Terry's criteria for the opposite sex were pretty simple and largely based on sensory attributes: how they looked, how their voices sounded, how sweet they smelled. She liked athletic men and was attracted by the way they talked or smiled. Hands, shoulders, lips, and eyes were all important to her, just like they were to most black women of the time. The clothing style of the time adopted by black men—known affectionately in the slang of the day as soul brothers—was intriguing in itself (to some): platform shoes, big hats, bell bottoms, tight pants, and an interesting display of chest hair.

While little is clear about Terry's relationships from those days, Terry McMillan was no different than the rest of the women of her generation.

Academically, Terry got good grades, enjoyed writing, and was writing a lot, enough to fill up suitcases. "Writing became an outlet for my dissatisfactions, distaste, and my way of trying to make sense of what was happening around me. It was my way of trying to fix what I thought was broken. It later became the only way to explore personally what I didn't understand."

One of the things Terry didn't understand, and wanted to explore, was where her mother got the strength to raise five children. Terry took the childhood experiences that were stored in her memories and began putting them on paper, writing about what she knew. She began writing a short story, set in a fictitious town named Point Haven, about a lusty black mother, Mildred

Peacock, struggling to raise her five children between her own relationships and marriages with an assortment of losers. "I wanted to show a middle-aged woman—black and for the most part deprived—who focused on raising her kids without really devoting any time to her life and her future. I wanted to show that in getting from point One to point Ten, she did enjoy making love, that she did know how to have a good time, and that she doesn't sit around and cry and whine. . . ."

But all the writing Terry did was for fun, not a career option. Terry still didn't have any goals, really couldn't think of a "normal" career path. She was feeling that familiar, dangerous feeling: boredom. "I came back from a ski trip where I'd done a lot of drinking, and I knew I had to do something. I pulled out a suitcase of my writing." She thought that perhaps there was a collection there that she could somehow get into print. But her efforts to do so had only limited success, except for publication in magazines like *Yardbird*.

While attending UC Berkeley, Terry met Clyde Taylor, then a professor of African American Studies there. Although she never took his class, they became friends, running into each other on campus as well as on the extremely active Bay Area literary scene. Occasionally, she invited Taylor and his wife to dinner, and visited them too.

"She tried to learn from me—she was so engaging, different from most students," Taylor remembers. "She was looking for the keys to how things worked. Her mentality was that of a grad student, with the attitude 'I'm gonna be out of here soon and I'm gonna do this with the information I've got.'

"With professors, most students have a formal attitude: I'll see him in his office. Terry would just start a conversation, friend to friend. She wasn't into a peer thing or the frat thing. She did seem to be searching. She asked for advice: 'What do you think about this or that?'

"I remember her writing poetry in those days and nibbling around a literary beginning. The poetry thing was there. She was shy about her literary potential. Although she had a way of being direct—she would come up and ask you any kind of question—about her literary talent she was quiet. She'd do readings of her poetry at various literary events. She wasn't that active but it meant a good deal to her. She didn't seem to push it hard—if someone asked her to she would. She was molding herself, and the Bay Area was a great environment for that in those days. Literary people would encourage each other. There was a Third World consciousness, the beginnings of feminism, and youth, plus the remainders of a counterculture.

"She had a long period of being friends with people who became famous. Ntozake Shange, Thulani Davis, Jessica Hagedorn. It was a very Third-Worldish scene. The circles she moved in were not strictly black or female.

"Terry is a poetic personality. I think that's where that creative thing comes from. But I suspect that she comes from a background where nobody expected anything from anybody. A rather vacuous background—not even discouraging. Just indifferent."

After graduating in 1976 with a bachelor's degree in journalism, Terry still had not arrived at a career decision. She continued to work in a rich suburb outside San Francisco as a typist while trying to decide what to do with her life. Two years later, in January 1978, Terry was living in San Anselmo, California. Still idealistic, she had been thinking long and hard and talking to friends and family about what to do next. Although she was happiest writing, she was aware of, and had to face, the cold, hard facts: It was damn hard for writers to make money off their writing.

Writing as a career, she believed, was for eccentrics—the kind who didn't mind living in a tiny studio too small to turn around in, and who were starving, of course. Having to steal other people's milk off their front steps. Who could make a habit out of putting on their one good suit (which looked best in dim light because it was so threadbare) and crashing fancy parties so they could eat. Who would write and write and write, then try to sell their work, and get rejection after rejection. Well, that was not in Terry's nature. No way. Even when she had lived in an underprivileged neighborhood, she had dismissed the idea that she'd have to stay in it the rest of her life. In her own way, Terry had already spoiled herself: She aimed high. But hanging out with writers, she'd heard the horror stories: They didn't get paid, they worked hard and had to hold down multiple jobs that left them little time for writing, on and on and on.

In a January 1978 letter to Ishmael Reed—who had become her mentor and with whom she had stayed in touch since graduation—Terry despaired that it was unlikely that she could support herself as a poet, playwright, or nonfiction writer, and certainly not a novelist because, she noted, she'd never finished a story longer than fifteen pages. Still, she wanted to publicly express her thoughts, feeling, and experiences in some way. Her decision, she stated to him, was that she would go to film school. The visual medium, she believed, was the best way for her to express herself in the way she wanted, to make a statement, to get respect and admiration—and to make a living. She asked Reed if he would write a letter of recommendation for her.

Terry's next stop was New York City and the Columbia University Film School, where she enrolled in the master's degree of fine arts program to study screenwriting.

Founded in 1754 as King's College, in 1897 Columbia University moved from forty-ninth Street and Madison Avenue, where it had stood for fifty years, to 116th Street and Broadway on the Upper West Side of Manhattan in the area known as Morningside Heights.

The idea behind the move was to place the university in an "urban academic village," in a more spacious setting. Designed by the architectural firm of McKim, Mead & White, the buildings on the new campus were modeled after those of the Italian Renaissance, and the campus is the largest single collection of McKim, Mead & White buildings in existence.

Over the years, Columbia's new location afforded it the prestige of a visual showpiece as well as a historic one. First, it was the oldest institution of higher learning in the state of New York and the fifth oldest in the United States. Second, it was architecturally important. The architectural centerpiece of the campus is Low Memorial Library, named in honor of the father of former university president Seth Low. Built in the Roman classical style, it appears in the New York City Register of Historic Places. The Library's broad flight of steps—which has been seen in many movies—descends to a large plaza, which has become a popular place for students to gather, and from there to College Walk, a promenade that bisects the central campus. And to the north of Low Library stands Pupin Hall, which in 1966 was designated a national historic landmark in recognition of the atomic research undertaken there by Columbia's scientists beginning in 1925. To the east is St. Paul's Chapel, which is listed with the New York City Register of Historic Places.

Other landmarks and historic sites within walking distance of the Columbia campus are the Cathedral Church of St. John the Divine, the world's largest Gothic-style cathedral; Grant's Tomb, a national historic site; and Riverside Park, which extends for over two miles along the Hudson River. (In September 1776, this was the site of the Battle of Harlem Heights in which George Washington led a Continental Army detachment to America's first victory as a nation.)

Morningside Heights—about twenty-five minutes from midtown Manhattan by subway—stretches from about 106th Street to about 123rd Street between Morningside Drive and Riverside Drive. From the top of a 135-foot bluff, it overlooks the Hudson River on one side and Harlem on the other. Formerly a neighborhood of poor people who lived in single-room occupancy buildings, the Heights was gentrified in the 1960s, some fifteen years before Terry's arrival. During her time at Columbia, the neighborhood had become a swanky area, with apartments on

Riverside Drive (known as the Gold Coast) selling for several hundreds of thousands of dollars.

According to the Columbia University bulletin, in 1916 the university became the first university to give a course in film. The 1979–80 course catalog from Columbia University School of the Arts listed the associates for film as Mikhail Baryshnikov, Warren Beatty, Paddy Chayefsky, E. L. Doctorow, Michael Douglas, Peter Falk, Buck Henry, Elia Kazan, Diane Keaton, Jerzy Kosinski, Arthur Krim, Sidney Lumet, Arthur Miller, Mike Nichols, Arthur Penn, Eric Pleskow, Mario Puzo, and Twyla Tharp.

In the first year, Terry and her fellow students were required to take the core master of fine arts curriculum plus electives, thereby being introduced to writing, directing, and the collaborative nature of filmmaking. At the end of the first year, in consultation with the faculty, each student would declare a concentration in a specific area, such as directing, producing, or history/theory/criticism. Of course, in Terry's case that was screenwriting.

The second year would be devoted to intensive work in the chosen concentration; as a screenwriting major, Terry would have to write a feature-length script. Then, at the end of the year, she would begin work on a thesis project, most likely a feature-length screenplay, which would be completed under the advisement of a faculty committee, and which must demonstrate originality of subject matter as well as mastery of the technique of cinematic and dramatic structure, characterization, and dialogue.

But Terry was not to complete the program. According to her accounts, she found the school to be "very racist," and quit just before completing the program. She later said that she and an African student—the only two blacks in the class—were not being treated right.

Finally, she was beginning to get the message. To see the handwriting on the wall. Which was:

STOP FIGHTING IT, DUMMY. WRITING IS WHAT YOU REALLY WANT TO DO. LET GO AND GET STARTED.

Falling back on her old standby, she registered with an employment agency that placed secretaries and typists and took a job as a word processor in a law firm so that she could make money while she concentrated on bringing her short stories to life.

3

············

The Writing Years

I don't write about victims. They just bore me to death.
I prefer to write about somebody who can pick themselves
back up and get on with their lives.

—Terry McMillan

In the late 1970s and early 1980s, a large high-profile law firm in New York City was almost a surreal place to work, especially for a young middle-class black woman from an economically disadvantaged neighborhood in the Midwest. Racially speaking, the most common breakdown was attorneys, white; secretaries and support staff, mixed; mailroom and copy center staff—well, let's just say that that's where the brothas and sistas could usually be found.

These kinds of law firms were actually a microcosm of the lifestyle of the affluent, and as such, could have a great influence—even if subliminal—upon anyone not of that world who got the chance to work inside such a firm. Antiques, plush carpeting, soft lighting, luxurious draperies, well-stocked cafeterias, were all part of the elements of comfort and abundance in these firms. There were always enough supplies to work with: pens, legal pads, file folders, highlighters. There were unlimited telephone calls and photocopying privileges. If you worked late, you could get a voucher to take a private car home. Or if you had to do an errand for your boss, you could get a private car to take you if it was really important.

Such firms were full of well-dressed men and women. The dress code was simple: You Better Look Damn Good. Elegant attire was always required, unless you were working on the weekend. On both the clients and the staff, you would see the best wool suits, coats, and socks. The smoothest silk ties and scarves. The most impeccable and stylish shoes. The finest leather briefcases and handbags. The sharpest haircuts, the most tasteful gold jewelry.

If the fashion parade was exciting, for anyone who enjoyed observing human nature, working in a law firm was heaven. Almost any overheard conversation would be a window into the world of those who had money, from "I'm going to the summer house this weekend" to "I'm picking up a refill for my Valium" to "I need to call my broker" to "Get me my mistress on the phone." Thus, it wasn't long before the reality of the profession and those at its heights tarnished any fantasies one may have had about the glamour of it.

Attorneys—and by extension, everyone else—would work around the clock. The legal profession is a time-sensitive business, and the transfer of information to another party has always been of utmost importance. But in the late 1970s, fax machines were not around except in such places as police stations, where

they would spit out pictures of suspects. Neither were computers, Federal Express, or other overnight mail services. Firms had
special accounts with messenger services or if a firm was of size,
would have an in-house messenger service. They had huge mail
rooms and copy centers, many of which operated around the
clock. If the firm had clients in other cities or countries, there
would often be several shifts. The law firm world was *not* a nine-
to-five one, and for those who recognized it, and had the necessary skills–as did Terry-there was a lot of money to be made.

There were a lot of practical skills to be learned too, free for
the absorbing. One extremely valuable lesson was all the different ways to write a letter. Attorneys correspond with each other,
their clients, and other parties in a fascinating way with plenty
of subtleties. There are occasions when you have to cover your
ass, explain something, give a warning, demand something, send
something, or request something. When such correspondence is
written, the understanding or the expectation is that it will most
likely be read by others (staff, boss, media, other attorney, judge,
jury), so the elements need to be carefully considered. A new
attorney takes a little while to do this, but after a while it becomes second nature. Anyone who works in a law firm and is
exposed to its correspondence is learning a valuable skill that can
be used forever.

And so it was into this world that Terry wisely took her su-
perior typing skills. She worked at a number of New York City
law firms, among them the soon-to-split-up Barovick Konecky
Braun Schwartz & Kay, then located at One Dag Hammarskjold
Plaza, within walking distance of the United Nations. Another

was Paterson, Belknap, Webb & Tyler, then at 30 Rockefeller Plaza. In those days, firms didn't change much. Partners stayed until they died, associates were hired, and the names stayed pretty much the same. Barovick et al was a rare exception; between 1979 and 1983, the firm changed names several times and eventually merged with another firm before disbanding permanently. But in the late 1970s, Barovick et al was one of the most powerful entertainment law firms, with clients like the Beach Boys, Casablanca Records, Neil Diamond, Bob Dylan, George Harrison, Steely Dan, Donna Summer, powerful managers, and a few other record labels and publishing companies.

Terry found her work enjoyable: She learned valuable lessons from the material she was handling (for example, at Barovick et al she learned how to read movie contracts), and made friends with the receptionists, switchboard operators, mailroom, messenger, and copy center staff. She would tell her co-workers that she had a manuscript and wanted someone to publish it, and regaled them with stories of the lifestyle and weather back in sunny California. She used the facilities, making phone calls and appointments—a privilege she was allowed because she was good at her job, so no one messed with her.

How good was she? She was so good that she edited the attorneys' documents, pointing out errors in style, sense, and continuity, and soon was the most-requested word processor in the place. They loved her.

And she was well paid. In 1983, Terry earned $15 an hour, and her average salary was $750 a week, sometimes $1,000. Being single, she could work shifts that no one else wanted: Frequently, after finishing her shift at one firm, she would take an assignment at another for a few hours.

At the time, Terry lived in a one-bedroom apartment in Brooklyn—complete with a few mice and lots of roaches—at 42 Fort Greene Place. The redbrick brownstone was in a busy downtown neighborhood known as Fort Greene. The Brooklyn Academy of Music, Pratt Institute, and the Lafayette Avenue Presbyterian Church (where, it is said, the Emancipation Proclamation was drafted), were all nearby, as was the thirty-acre Fort Greene Park. Fort Greene Place, Terry's block, was a shady, tree-lined street of well kept brownstones, east of Flatbush Avenue, behind the Brooklyn Academy of Music and near Long Island University. Brooklyn Technical High School (known locally as Brooklyn Tech) was across the street from Terry's building, and the downtown shopping area was a few blocks away.

A few doors down, an almost identical brownstone—number 48—had been converted into a rooming house. In that rooming house lived a thirtyish black construction worker named Leonard Welch, who often used his carpenter skills to make extra money. In 1982 he was hired to install wooden floors in number 42 Fort Greene Place.

When Terry saw the two-hundred-twenty-five pounds of this six four, tall, dark, muscular, mustached black man installing floors in her building, she wanted some of that—protruding ears and all.

Leonard Welch was the only son in his single-parent family, which consisted of his mother, Willie Welch; a twin sister, Valerie; and an older sister, Sylvia. Leonard was very close to Valerie, who had a history of emotional problems, including suicidal tendencies; she had even spent some time at Bellevue Hospital. Although Welch had dropped out of high school in the eleventh grade, he later got his high school equivalency diploma. To keep in shape, he worked those muscles at the gym at least three days a week.

Welch also had a wife, Jammer Ballard-Welch, from whom he was separated. Jammer, together with their children, lived across Fort Greene Park in the Walt Whitman projects.

Over on Fort Greene Place, Terry and Leonard worked their magic on each other, and they fell in love. Leonard soon moved out of the rooming house at number 48 into Terry's apartment at number 42. So began a three-year relationship, during which he was occasionally employed as a construction worker and in between construction gigs, used his carpentry and woodworking skills to make additional money. For their apartment, he built furniture and crafted sculptures, as well as shelves, a wall unit, and a bed frame. The two lovers soon moved a few streets over into another apartment in a brownstone at 100 Bergen Street, another quiet, tree-lined block which was part of the Boerum Hill Historic District of the New York City Landmarks Preservation Commission.

But their relationship was stormy. Terry was a tough mama who knew where she was headed. Like her mother, she didn't pull any punches; she was outspoken, bold, loud, and knew how to get what she had to get. Terry was working hard and making plenty of money; both the work and the dollars rolled in almost effortlessly. The phone would ring, the agency would request her, and out she'd go to make more money. Leonard, at the other extreme, was working hard, struggling to establish himself. But construction work was sporadic, he would frequently be laid off, and his financial situation was often uncertain; once, Terry even had to lend him money so he could take her to the movies on her birthday. Although that didn't matter to Terry (she loved him), Leonard's bruised ego would rise up, mix with his frustration, and he would take it all out on her. There were many arguments, the first of which centered around a revealing bathing suit Terry wore. One summer, when Terry and Leonard went to Saratoga Springs, New York, to the Newport Jazz Festival, he slapped her in the face after a big argument.

Still, Terry stayed with him, perhaps unconsciously doing what her mother did, either because she believed in him or she didn't want to believe the handwriting on the wall, the clues, the clear messages, that he was not good for her and that this was not how a woman was supposed to be treated.

Whether she realized the karma or not, Terry was unhappy and definitely not thriving in this damaged environment. She was still sucking down that tequila and putting that cocaine up her nose. "I had what I considered to be a drinking problem," she said in an interview. "I couldn't drink—a couple of drinks and I was drunk—but I didn't know it and it took me four years to realize it. I didn't drink every day, you didn't see me stumbling. But it was a problem and I couldn't handle it."

If they called Terry in to work and it had been a wild night, she'd have to tell a white lie about having an emergency like lost keys or broken plumbing and that she'd be in, only a little bit later. This would buy her enough time to sober herself up and come in straight. Ever confident, though, she would square this by noting that some of the people she worked with were no strangers to hangovers themselves.

But there soon came a time, she says, when she looked in the mirror and saw her father. Realizing that she needed to take herself seriously, she decided she would kick her addictions to the two substances. She has never said exactly how.

Terry was still writing short stories, and had been working on the one inspired by her mother, which she named "Mama." Although she had little time to devote to her writing she was so involved in her story that she worked on it whenever she could. Her usual routine was to get up in when it was still dark—about four-thirty in the morning—and write for four hours or so. The quiet of the early morning hours was what she loved, and her writing was done in complete silence. Music, she had found, was a distraction: She had tried having jazz or classical music playing but it just didn't work. Often her characters would come to her in dreams. And then she would expand on them. "It's like there's this friendship that I'm starting to develop, and I have to get to know these people more. Why is the character in this situation that I already know he or she is? And then I start probing, and I start looking everywhere I can for information about somebody who would do the kind of stuff that I have them do."

While riding the subway to work a few hours later, she would edit her new draft in red pen. Fortunately, new technology was making work on her project even easier: A revolutionary tool, the desktop computer, was making its debut in the workplace (or at least the ones that realized the value of, and could afford, such state-of-the-art equipment). And law firms were among those workplaces. (Computers would not be widely owned by individuals for a few years yet.) So Terry could type her work on the computer at the office, save it onto a big fat 5 ¼" floppy disk, and make changes to the saved work until it was right. No more correction fluid, no more cutting and pasting. A technological miracle, indeed! So, during down time at the office, she would type in the changes and print it out on her lunch hour. "All my co-workers would come up to me and say, 'The laser printer's full of your shit,' " she has said. "Everybody was on my side."

So finally, after years of being transported by the words of others, and having a story she wanted to get published, Terry seriously set her mind to seeing what connections she could make in the writing and publishing world. She pursued every outlet she could find that might provide her with time—and money—to write. She made it her business to educate herself about the world of writers and writing. She read writer's magazines, such as *Writer's Digest* and *The Writer,* which not only contained articles full of tips on the craft of writing, but listed places where writers could send and sell their work. She got ideas from articles that profiled writers, and addresses from articles that mentioned writer's organizations, meetings and conferences. She read *Coda* magazine, published by an organization called Poets and Writers. For her personal reference library, she bought books on writers and writing. In short, she established a foundation for herself. She also met lots of people in the New York City writing community. She kept in touch with her writing friends, especially Ishmael Reed, with whom she corresponded regularly and sent copies of her work.

Although she loved Leonard, their life together was a little too traumatic, and now that she was serious about being a writer Terry needed a quiet place to write. Through the writer's publications she was reading and by word of mouth from other writers, Terry learned about artists' colonies.

Artists' colonies exist all over the world. They provide room and board for periods of one week to seven months to highly talented creative artists who can take a short leave from daily responsibilities to work on a specific project. The most valuable aspect of these colonies is that their naturally beautiful and peaceful settings also provide artists with the sorely needed solitude, freedom from distraction, and companionship among peers that help lead to their best work. Some colonies offer total quiet and seclusion, while others have readings, workshops, and concerts.

To get into an artists' colony, the only requirement is talent; age, race, nationality, and ability to pay for residency are not factors. Applicants send information and work samples, which are reviewed by a panel of experts in the applicable discipline. Most colonies are nonprofit corporations whose operating budgets consists of gifts, grants, and bequests.

One colony that caught Terry's eye was Yaddo, located in Saratoga Springs, New York.

Yaddo is a beautiful, wooded estate of four hundred acres on which stands a fifty-five-room mansion, three smaller houses, studio buildings, and a building for administrative offices and maintenance shops. There are also four small lakes and a famous rose garden, which is the only part of the property open to the public.

The property originally housed a farm, gristmill, and tavern operated by a Revolutionary War veteran named Jacobus Barhyte. He built his house on a little hill from which he could enjoy a view of the battlefield where he had fought, and at his tavern dined many well-known writers of the 1830s and 1840s, including Edgar Allan Poe.

In 1881 Spencer Trask, a New York City financier, and his wife Katrina, a poet, bought the property, naming it Yaddo at their small daughter's suggestion. When the main residence burned to the ground ten years later, the Trasks built another mansion, which became the scene of famous house parties attended by artists, authors, composers, statesmen, and industrialists. After the deaths of their four children left them without heirs, the Trasks decided "to found a permanent Home to which shall come from time to time . . . authors, painters, sculptors, musicians and other artists both men and women . . . whom we would have enjoy the hospitality of Yaddo, their sole qualification being that they have done, are doing, or give promise of doing good and earnest work." In 1900 they formed the corporation of Yaddo, and the first group of artists arrived in 1926.

At Yaddo, the rule is that the hours between 9:00 A.M. and 4:00 P.M., and after 10:00 P.M., are quiet hours, when artists work without interruption from either fellow residents or outside guests. One of the quiet colonies, Yaddo does not arrange or encourage workshops, readings, recitals, performances, exhibitions, or other activities. For recreation, there are winding roads and paths through the woods, a tennis court, swimming pool, pool table, Ping-Pong table, and bicycles. Breakfast and dinner are taken communally, while lunch is packed for each artist to carry to his or her studio.

This all sounded like heaven to Terry, who applied to Yaddo for a residency in 1982, and spent two weeks there. She would visit Yaddo again in 1983 and 1986.

In the spring of 1983, Terry was accepted to another popular artist's colony: the MacDowell Colony in Peterborough, New Hampshire. MacDowell colonists have won more than fifty Pulitzer prizes and seven MacArthur Foundation Genius Awards. Like Terry, many of them were not yet known when they first came to MacDowell. Terry spent a peaceful forty-four days there, from April 15 to May 29.

The MacDowell Colony was founded in 1907. In 1896, composer Edward MacDowell bought a farm in Peterborough, New Hampshire, to rest and work in tranquility. There, he said, he was able to triple his creative activity. He hoped that, by expanding the facilities, his farm might become a workplace for other artists. Although he died in 1908, in 1906 a fund had been started in his honor by many prominent people of his time, among them Grover Cleveland, Andrew Carnegie, Victor Herbert, Henry Van Dyke, and J. Pierpont Morgan. This fund was used by his widow to found the MacDowell Colony.

The colony has 450 acres of woodlands and fields, and forty-two supporting buildings. It welcomes thirty-one artists in summer and about twenty-two in heated studios during other seasons, with the average length of a residency being six weeks. Almost no MacDowell studio is within sight of another, and each is simply but comfortably furnished. Breakfast and dinner are served family-style in the main dining room. Lunches, packed in picnic baskets, are left on studio doorsteps before noon. Telephone messages are delivered only in emergencies.

Other artists who had residencies at MacDowell were Leonard Bernstein, Willa Cather, Aaron Copland, Studs Terkel, Alice Walker, Jules Feiffer, and James Baldwin, who once wrote:

I will be very glad . . . to be working at the Colony—which for many years now has lived in my mind as a refuge and a workshop and the place in which I most wanted to be when the time comes, as it perpetually does, to crouch in order to spring.

According to the 1983 MacDowell newsletter, forty-nine artists arrived for residencies between early February and early May. They included sixteen visual artists, three filmmakers, seven composers, and twenty-three writers. Among the writers were Claude Brown, author of *Manchild in the Promised Land* (1965), who was completing a book on "the 33-year heroin addiction epidemic in America," Mary Higgins Clark, who was working on her fifth novel, and Audre Lorde, who was completing a collection of essays and working on a sequence of poems. Terry, the newsletter noted, was working on "a collection of short stories about black women and men, and on a novel." Her photo was included in the newsletter.

After the residencies at Yaddo and MacDowell, Terry had expanded her short story into over four hundred pages, the first draft of what eventually became *Mama*.

One Sunday, Terry was watching the television program *Like It Is,* hosted by black journalist Gil Noble. His guests were the authors Maya Angelou and John Oliver Killens, members of a group called the Harlem Writers Guild. Terry decided to check out this organization.

Founded soon after World War II by Killens (who was a writing mentor to several generations), Rosa Guy, and John Henrik Clarke, the group has nurtured such writers as Paule Marshall, Ossie Davis, Louise Merriwether, Wesley Brown, Brenda Wilderson, Walter Dean Myers, and many others. It still exists today, and informal estimates suggest that members have written well over a hundred books.

"It was a beacon light for those of us in American publishing at that time," says longtime member Sarah Elizabeth Wright, author of *This Child's Gonna Live* (1970). "We cried to each other. None of the writers felt they were alone. Other members at various times were Walter Christmas, Audre Lorde. Irvin Burgie, who wrote the Barbados national anthem and the banana boat song. Harry Belafonte was a guest at our meetings. Ossie Davis wrote *Purlie Victorious* while a member. Lonnie Elder wrote *Sounder* while a member. Bill Tatum (who would become the editor of the *Amsterdam News*), who was working for Swedish newspapers at the time. Alice Childress, the playwright. We were all poor black writers who wanted to write! I remember many who rented typewriters or got them from the Salvation Army.

"A lot of our members lived alone, in single-room occupancy hotels, and so forth. But some got a little better off. We could always get in touch with each other. We were working-class writers. Gutsy writers. We were so put out by this discrimination—our parents and grandparents had endured terrible things. We shared the details of our humiliations.

"Between 1980 and 1985 we met at the homes of Rosa Guy (Riverside Drive), John Oliver Killens (Brooklyn) occasionally, mine (West End Avenue), and Bill Williams Forde (Park West Village). Bill didn't always have an apartment—he used to live in an SRO hotel. We'd meet every Monday night for two hours, minimum. If somebody was really hot or something was really popping, we'd stay later, sometimes till 11. Year in and year out. We had a Christmas/New Year's party every year. The work was always supported.

"Terry was very talkative, young and full of energy. She read at the meetings at Bill Williams Forde's house. I thought there was growth needed and that she would acquire that. The content was very appealing, especially to women who sit around and talk about life as they are experiencing it."

Says mystery author Grace Edwards *(In the Shadow of the Peacock):* "Terry was in the Harlem Writers Guild in the mid-eighties. We used to meet at Bill Williams Forde's apartment in Park West Village on Central Park West. The group varied, from twelve to fifteen people at most, because Bill's apartment wasn't that large."

The late Bill Williams Forde, who wrote the novel *The Children of Annabella,* joined almost at the very start and directed the Guild for much of the seventies and early eighties. He once said, "We needed a guild to compare notes in order to write anything. Who are we? What is our language? Do we write like Henry James? Shakespeare? Thomas Mann? We were searching for our experience and our language."

But, says Grace Edwards, "It probably got to be a strain on Bill. He wasn't in the best of health. He passed away several years ago." She continues about Terry. "Terry had a very exuberant style. The responses [of the group to her work] were good. She was a very generous person. Later, she did not hesitate to refer me to her agent, Diane Cleaver. Diane said, 'Terry told me about you and it's true, your work is good. I'd like to represent you.' And for *In The Shadow of the Peacock,* Terry took the time to give me a beautiful quote."

During one of the group's sessions, Terry read *Mama,* which was then a short story, to her fellow members.

"After I finished reading, the room got real quiet," Terry later said in an interview. "Finally somebody said, 'That doesn't sound like a short story to me. It sounds like the beginning of a novel. You sure can write!'"

Another writer Terry met in the Harlem Writers Guild was Doris Jean Austin, a large, outgoing woman who had had an extremely turbulent life. Terry and Doris soon became close.

Doris had grown up in a small New Jersey town. One Saturday when she was twelve years old, Doris went into a store to buy her first pair of nylon stockings to wear to church the next day. As she walked out of the store, she was suddenly, brutally grabbed and shoved into the backseat of a car. The car radio was playing an Ike and Tina Turner song. While one man held her arms down, the other raped her. Doris was horrified to recognize both of them as her neighbors—one of them, she knew, was married, and his wife was pregnant. When she finally got away by slipping her arms out of her coat, they yelled after her, "Come and get your coat, girl. Nobody's going to believe you, you know. Nobody!"

The men were eventually caught. But the community's stares were too much for Doris. She had to transfer to another high school, where she developed a tough shell and learned to be a survivor. In fact, she suppressed her memories of the rape for more than twenty years. When she turned eighteen, she begged her mother to let her join the Women's Army Corps, where she began her college education. But the military was not the place for Doris, and she was later court-martialed for going AWOL. When she learned that she could get an early discharge if she was married, "I became engaged, married, and exercised my married woman's option to become a civilian again," she wrote.

As the proceedings of Doris Jean's second divorce were moving along, she received some terrible news: Her mother had been diagnosed with cancer. The twenty-nine-year old Doris Jean traveled often from her apartment in Manhattan to visit her hospitalized mother in Jersey City, up until her mother died.

Her mother's death was a crushing blow to Doris Jean, who turned to alcohol to numb her pain and grief. But by the end of that year, there was another blow: Doris Jean herself was diagnosed with cancer. Her reaction was a kind of relief: Life had been so damned cruel anyway, she reasoned. So she put her affairs in order, gave away her possessions, and "surrendered myself to Memorial Sloan Kettering Cancer Institute . . . prepared to die, as my grandmother and my mother before me had died, of cancer."

But Doris Jean didn't die. When she was released from the hospital, not yet thirty years old, she had to start all over again. She sought professional help, and during therapy, her memories of the rape resurfaced and were faced. And one of the things she did to put her wounded self back together, was to write.

Doris Jean Austin had written a story that began with a Harlem drug dealer being killed by a bow and arrow. After working on it with the Harlem Writers Guild in 1979, she changed it to the story of a young black family in 1950s Jersey City. Its main character, Elzina Tompkins, searches for fulfillment and happiness while trying to please both her proud and righteous grandmother Rosalie, the woman who raised her, and her wild, handsome childhood sweetheart, Jesse James, who becomes her husband. In 1987, the New American Library published this novel, called *After the Garden,* to glowing reviews.

"We were all black, we were all young, and we were all trying to tell stories we thought worth telling," remembers Terry.

In 1986, several members of the Harlem Writers Guild, including Doris Jean Austin, formed their own group called the

New Renaissance Writers Guild, which is still in existence to-day. Other New Renaissance Writers Guild alumni include Akua Lezli Hope, a New York poet who gave readings to audiences in colleges, prisons, parks, museums, restaurants, and bars; Baron James Ashanti, also a poet, who helped create the black literature panels at the Third National Writers Congress held in New York City in 1980; and Memphis native Arthur Flowers, a Vietnam veteran and blues singer whose *De Mojo Blues* was published that year, 1986. Doris Jean went on to teach journalism and fiction, in both workshop and classroom settings.

Terry was finding her writing voice. Not surprisingly, it was the same kind of writing that had formed her poetry: about people and their relationships.

"My focus has been on women who basically fall in love with losers, who aren't nurturing. Too many women—and my mother was one of them—are too nurturing and go all out of their way for their husbands and their kids, but I've not seen as many men go all out of their way for us," she has said.

"I'm just really interested in how people treat each other, and how our internal clocks sort of decide what happens to us externally. How we deal with ourselves from the inside out, and how we interact with each other. I'm really particularly interested not just in men and women, but parents and children and just relationships between people where there is this yin and yang and stuff going on, where people don't cooperate, or they misunderstand each other, or mistreat each other."

At home, Leonard Welch alternated between encouragement

of and jealousy toward Terry's writing. "His ego was ruptured," Terry said.

From all accounts, it sounds as if Leonard was frustrated at his own lack of success. Imagine: He did carpentry but was not making a lot of money at it. He had no real place of his own to live. He didn't have lots of possessions. He had children from whose mother he was estranged. The work he did get from construction was sporadic and depended on the will of Mother Nature. So every day for him was a challenge: How will it turn out? Will I get paid? Will I get ripped off? And even for a person who is content with the status quo, being thwarted at every opportunity when you think things will be better is psychically tiring and takes a toll.

Perhaps for Welch to see Terry have a dream, latch onto it, and do the necessary things to make it happen was frustrating to him as a man. Men are supposed to be driven like that, not women, and even if women are, the men are supposed to be even more driven. And—at least up to that point, as evidenced by where he was in his life—Welch had not been able to make very much happen, despite his efforts. It is even possible that in his mind, his chosen field—working with his hands—was something far more saleable (because of its tangibility) than writing. Yet Terry was pursuing it. And even letting serendipity happen.

Nevertheless, in the summer of 1983, a few months after she had returned from the peace and quiet of the MacDowell Colony, Terry became pregnant.

4

Crouching in Order to Spring

I am tired of carrying this plantation on my shoulders . . . I'm not trying to prove anything to white folks, and I'm not trying to make them feel guilty—my editor didn't enslave my ancestors.

—Terry McMillan

The writer's world is a strange place.

Most books about writers and writing will either talk about the writer's craft, and/or analyze the written work (that is, the result of the craft). Beyond that, there is the actual business of writing—a craft in itself!—which if learned well, can help the writer elevate her work from mere craft to a commodity, that is, something that is deemed valuable and worth paying for.

There is another element, though. A pretty important element, in fact, for a writer to be familiar with, but at the same time the most mysterious one and the hardest one to get a handle on. That element is the publishing industry. Much like the music industry is the farthest thing from the musician's mind as he composes his tunes, the book publishing industry is the farthest from the writer's consciousness as she slaves away trying to birth a story. Especially a first-time novelist.

This was true in Terry McMillan's case, too. Except that Terry was a focused person, who knew what she wanted and was not intimidated by stories of failure. Armed with that attitude, she was about to change the face of the book publishing industry.

The writings of black folks have been published since at least the early 1800s, but back then they appeared mostly in black newspapers for a black audience. Before slavery was abolished, most of these publications, of course, were based in the northern states, where slavery had been eliminated since the late 1700s. This black press began with the first black newspaper, *Freedom's Journal,* edited and published by Samuel Cornish and John B. Russwurm in New York. Its first issue appeared on March 16, 1827. Other newspapers with names like *Rights of All, Colored American,* and *Mirror of Liberty* sprang up in New York City over the next ten years, as did publications in Philadelphia, Cleveland, and San Francisco. Their titles were indicative of their content, which was advocacy of freedom for black citizens. The first issue of *The North Star,* published by the famous abolitionist Frederick Douglass, appeared in Rochester, New York, on December 3, 1847.

After the Civil War, the black press grew and has never stopped. Then as now, its purpose is to keep the black community informed of political and social issues that affect it. It exposes political injustice and corruption that have an impact on the black community, and demands redress. It announces and records achievements of black people in all areas of business, religion, education, and social life, which would most likely be overlooked by the white press. It announces and records the activities of both national and local black organizations. It gives its black readers a forum for expressing their opinions, suggestions, and solutions to any current issues. In short, it provides a way for black people to become more aware of their own achievements and opportunities.

So there was certainly a lot of black writing going on, at least in the newspaper world.

As for the book world . . . well, let us first briefly examine the book publishing industry.

For over a hundred years, the book publishing industry was traditionally run by wealthy white families who passed control of their companies from generation to generation. As an industry, publishing in America began in the 1800s when a young printer named Matthew Carey came to Philadelphia from Dublin, Ireland. Using a British company as a prototype, Carey established the first general publishing house. Over the next fifty years, several American publishing companies were established: Harper & Brothers in 1817; John Wiley & Sons in 1828; Little, Brown & Company in 1837; Charles Scribner's Sons in 1846; and Houghton Mifflin Company in 1849. In the United States, the hub of the publishing business was New York City.

The family-owned aspect of the major publishing companies was threatened after 1950, when the tremendous growth of the publishing business led to a need for new capital. That new capital was acquired through mergers and the sale of company stock to the public. Indeed, between 1958 and 1970, 307 pub-lishing company mergers were executed. (Some industry cynics might read that as "307 publishing companies were executed.") The breakdown: 224 mergers were among publishers them-selves, thirty-three were with other communications companies, and twenty-two were with companies that had nothing to do with publishing or communications. By 1980, though, some of those corporations, having no knowledge or interest in the book industry and suffering because of it, had begun to sell off their publishing interests. In the mideighties there was a new flood of corporate mergers; and in the 1990s, foreign-owned corpora-tions acquired several major American publishers, creating what some industry insiders complained of as an oligopoly.

What goes on in these publishing houses? There are three cat-egories of books that publishing companies publish. The first category, and the one most people are familiar with, is what the industry calls trade books, that is, fiction and nonfiction books for the general reader. These books include novels, biographies, travel guides, cookbooks, do-it-yourself books, picture books for children, books on current affairs, history, or psychology—in other words, the books you'd buy in a general bookstore. Although trade books are the books that get the most visibility and hype (they are displayed and sold in bookstores, advertised and reviewed in newspapers, on television, radio, and the In-ternet, and reported on the best-seller lists) the fact is that trade books make up only 25 percent of a publishing house's total output. The rest is made up of the second category of books:

educational books and reference books (dictionaries, encyclopedias, textbooks, and so on), and the third category which is called mass-market books. These are softcover or hardcover books which are developed and sold to larger audiences than a bookstore can reach. These are the books we see in places such as supermarkets, drugstores, newsstands, stationery stores, airports, and department stores.

When a completed manuscript is received at a publishing house, it is taken over by the editor, who works closely with the author to polish up the work. Then, copy editors correct spelling and grammar, check accuracy of the facts, and prepare the book for the typesetter. The designer plans the book's format—determines the size of the pages, the type style and size, and lays out the pages and the artwork. The book is then set in type.

Meanwhile, plans for advertising and distributing the book are already in the works. Catalogs listing and describing forthcoming books are sent to bookstores, libraries, consumers, and others to solicit advance sales or commitments to buy. This information helps the publisher determine how many copies to print (known as the print run). Accountants estimate the amount of money that the publisher should spend on advertising and promoting the book. The degree of that effort and budget will depend on the size of the house and the importance of the book.

Large publishers have their own sales staff, who are briefed by editors at sales conferences before they go on the road. On the road, trade books are sold primarily by salespersons visiting bookstores across the country and taking orders for the forthcoming books. As part of their promotional strategy, publishers may provide advance copies (that is, copies of the book released prior to the official publication date) of a book to influential personalities (such as political figures or celebrities) who might plug the book to the public. The publisher may also send the author on tours of bookstores to autograph copies for customers. Researchers watch the progress of sales to determine if and when the publisher should order another printing. The process of physically getting the books from the publisher to the bookseller is known as distribution. This is achieved in large part by whole-sale book distributors, which is an industry unto itself.

Most early black American literature fell into two broad categories. One was the autobiographical narrative by former slaves, the aim of which was to show a human black face to white America. The other type of black literature emulated the general literature of the time, as in the case of the Senegalese slave and poet Phillis Wheatley, whose style and themes are closer to Anglo-Saxon than African. Perhaps this was a way to disprove the theory that blacks were inferior. And there was some early black literature which took on religious tones, such as that of poet Jupiter Hammon, a slave whose work was dismissed by critics who considered it too pious and forced, written to affirm (for the benefit of their masters) that slaves were perfectly content in their world of devout subservience.

The first published novel written by a black American was *Clotel, or, The President's Daughter: A Narrative of Slave Life in the United States* by William Wells Brown, a fugitive slave. This 104-page volume was published in 1853 by James Redfaith of Boston, and sold for ten cents. It was an antislavery novel about one of Thomas Jefferson's children by his slave mistress Sally Hemings. In 1859, the novel *Our Nig* by Harriet E. Wilson was published, probably the first novel written by an African American woman.

From the years following Reconstruction until the 1920s, the bulk of black American writing seemed to be aimed at proving that even if they couldn't afford all the material trappings, blacks had the same middle-class attitudes, morals, and principles as whites. But once the 1920s came—the United States had just emerged from a world war, things were looking up, attitudes were changing—black literature went in the opposite direction: no more polite, conservative, predictable writing featuring smiling, grinning, dancing, docile characters. There was going to be some in-your-face blackness in this writing, take it or leave it.

Thus began the Harlem Renaissance, the period during the 1920s when a large number of black poets, writers, artists, musicians, and performers expressed themselves and their experiences as blacks in America through their work. Writers and poets such as Countee Cullen, W. E. B. Du Bois, Jessie Fauset, Rudolph Fisher, Langston Hughes, Zora Neale Hurston, James Weldon Johnson, Claude McKay, and Jean Toomer, educated the black and white public about being black in America and expressed a new pride in that blackness. Critic Alain Locke chronicled a collection of their writings in the 1925 anthology *The New Negro,* and continued to promote writers who had outgrown what he called "the pathetic overcompensation of a group inferiority complex." His attitude was that it was about time for black writers to stop trying to get whites to love them, use their creativity to express their true feelings on their blackness, and let the reader decide (or go to hell, whichever was applicable). More books were published by black authors during the 1920s than any other previous decade in American history.

For the most part, the literary establishment in the United States—publishers, editors, critics, and professors—has been made up of white people. Their tastes and backgrounds determine which authors are published, promoted, and praised. Unless they were very liberal, or progressive, or someone turned them on to black authors or issues, black authors or black issues were not very widely published until the civil rights movement of the 1960s, which was the catalyst for much activist writing. Major publishing houses then became eager to publish the essays, plays, poetry, and novels of black writers who expressed their experiences as an oppressed people in the land of the free, home of the brave.

Much of the important black literature of the late 1960s was protest literature, written by men—men who wrote about ghetto life, prison life, and racism. Among these male writers were Eldridge Cleaver, George Jackson, LeRoi Jones (later known as Imamu Amiri Baraka), James Baldwin, Richard Wright, and Ralph Ellison, and their work had thought-provoking and controversial titles like *Prelude to a 20-Volume Suicide Note* (LeRoi Jones), *Manchild in the Promised Land* (Claude Brown), and *Die Nigger Die* (H. Rap Brown). Noted best-sellers in nonfiction from that period included *Black Rage* (William H. Grier and Price M. Cobbs), *Soul on Ice* and *Black Power,* (Eldridge Cleaver). John Oliver Killens's novel *And Then We Heard the*

Thunder was nominated for a Pulitzer prize in 1964, the year it was published.

The short list of black authors and poets of the 1960s and 1970s would include Nikki Giovanni, Maya Angelou, Gwendolyn Brooks, Alice Childress, Ernest J. Gaines, June Jordan, Toni Morrison, Ishmael Reed, Alice Walker, and John Edgar Wideman. There was a lot of good black literature of that time: serious, political, protesting, militant, in-your-face, edifying, thought-provoking. The black community, and the white community, were getting a concentrated course in Afrocentrism. This, then, was black literature.

"It seemed to be a period when you couldn't publish enough," said literary agent Marie Brown, who began her career in the publishing industry in 1967 as an editorial trainee at Doubleday. Needless to say, she was one of the few blacks in the publishing industry at the time. "During that period I was responsible for working on black books, as were most of the black people in publishing," she explained.

By the end of the 1970s, though, the protest theme had been pretty much worked to death. Many black writers began to write books for children and young adults, using black themes and settings. The work of black poets and novelists also continued to be published, as did that of black playwrights, who also had many of their contemporary plays produced on stage. A few black writers wrote science fiction works. Biographies and autobiographies were written about many of the famous black writers, and the works of Harlem Renaissance authors such as Richard Wright and Zora Neale Hurston were reintroduced and republished. And black women writers got a boost from the white feminist movement and publishing houses that specialized in the work of women writers.

Then, there was Alex Haley's *Roots,* published in 1976. Its success began a never-before-seen surge of interest and research into black ancestry, genealogy, and history, and inspired a flood of black biographies and autobiographies. Historical novels and plays such as *The Chaneysville Incident* and *The Brownsville Raid* were written. Both black and white people researched and wrote regional histories of blacks, which were published by independent or university presses.

In the 1980s, a few authors, such as Angelou, Morrison, Walker, and Gloria Naylor seemed to be the most visible black authors around, and in some cases their writings were analyzed and discussed in college literature courses. Walker's *The Color Purple* and Naylor's *The Women of Brewster Place* enjoyed huge success and were both turned into films.

Most American parents—black or other—in the fifties, sixties, seventies, and even eighties would have wept if their children expressed aspirations to be a writer. "Why don't you get a real job? You can't possible make any money off that" would have been the concerned reaction.

And they would have been right. Writing is a hard career to make money off. But even before it becomes a career, it must be developed, over hundreds of hours, as a craft—whether it is fiction or nonfiction writing. And while it requires next to no equipment (something to write with and something to write on), it does require time, commitment, quiet, and peace. Most authors must spend hundreds of hours perfecting their skills before they can sell one page of their work. The writer must not only write, but must also break from that writing to read, and when the time is right, to meet other writers to share work and receive critiques. Later, when confidence is achieved or the muse is turbulently struggling to break free, the writer must find a quiet place to write, to produce. Finally, when the work is ready for exposure, the writer must find someone, somewhere, to publish it.

Clearly, that is a full-time job in itself.

It was in this industry climate that Terry McMillan exposed her writing.

On April 24, 1984, Terry McMillan gave birth, by the natural method, to a baby boy she named Solomon Welch. Her water broke when she and Leonard, who was then unemployed, were playing Scrabble; Leonard was present in the delivery room. She asked Doris Jean Austin to be Solomon's godmother.

But finally Terry was seeing the handwriting on the wall for the relationship: "I knew things weren't working out and I was going to have to get rid of this man." She was thirty-two years old. She would leave Leonard less than a year later.

Meanwhile, *Mama* had been languishing, untouched for the most part. Finally, Terry took things into her own hands. She gathered up all the short stories she had written and sent them to Houghton Mifflin. (Houghton, who had published Ann Petry's novel *The Street* in 1946, also granted Petry a Houghton Mifflin Literary Fellowship. The Fellowship, founded in 1935 and awarded periodically, is designed to reward its own authors for a first adult trade book of outstanding literary merit.) "I decided I had nothing to lose by sending [them the] stories," Terry said. "I thought, maybe I'll get some free editorial advice." In her cover letter, she casually mentioned that she had written a novel.

Houghton responded that although they loved the stories, a collection would be difficult to sell. However, they inquired about the novel, and asked to see it. Terry was shocked . . . but she felt the fear and sent it anyway (as her mama would say). It was still in draft form, since she hadn't been focusing on it.

"About four days later I got an answer—it seemed I'd just dropped it in the mail. They said, 'We love it!' and made an offer to buy the book and publish it in hardcover.

"I freaked out. I got knots in my stomach at the thought of how much I had to revise." But she did it anyway: Rising at 4:30 A.M. she sat at her typewriter in her bathrobe, rewriting and revising, sometimes more than a dozen times, until it was time to get ready to go to work and take Solomon to the baby-sitter. She continued rewriting while waiting for the train. "Sometimes I'd let five or six trains go by," she says.

Lawrence Kessenich was an editor at the Boston-based Houghton Mifflin when the manuscript of *Mama* showed up. He had been in publishing for eight years at the time. A colleague of his named Dell Hammond was responsible for taking the first look at manuscripts to see whether they deserved to be read at all, he says. "If she found something that she thought was pretty good, she would generally read the whole thing. And Terry's was one of them. Dell read it and she came to me because she knew I did a lot of fiction. She said, 'I think this has really got something. It's kind of rough, it's kind of raw as far as the way it's written, but it's really authentic and really got a lot of power to it, and captures a segment of life that you don't see written about that much, daily life in a black urban community.' And I read it and felt exactly the same way she did, that it really had a very strong distinctive voice, and captured a sense of what that world was like in a way that I found very strong and very appealing.

"[By rough], she just meant that it needed a little work, which is not uncommon for a first novelist. I'm sure there was some stuff with punctuation, etc., and to be perfectly honest it's a little hard for me to remember where the roughness was, but it was really nothing that made it all that different from a lot of first novels.

"So I talked to Terry, I don't really remember that clearly that initial conversation, but of course she was very excited and quite interested. And you know the routine of a publishing house, I had to give it to a lot of other people to read. And those people liked it and thought it was worth taking on.

"So we took it on. I can't recall the exact figure, but it was a fairly typical advance for a first novel that you didn't expect to be something that was going to break out of the pack in some big way, so it was around $4,000 or $5,000, something like that. That was thirteen or fourteen years ago, so it sounds a lot worse now. I mean it wasn't that great then either, but that was typical for a first novel. I think at that point Terry thought it was okay.

"I told her she should get an agent so she would know what

the general situation was with first novels. So she got an agent, Diane Cleaver."

Born in Birmingham, England, Diane Cleaver was affiliated with the Sanford J. Greenburger literary agency on Fifth Avenue in Manhattan. Her career in publishing had begun at Doubleday, where she'd worked her way up from editorial assistant to editor; she later became an editor at Straight Arrow Books, Charles Scribner's Sons, and Simon & Schuster. In 1978, she formed her own literary agency affiliated with the Greenburger agency. Her clients were British and American authors, including John Fowles, Fay Weldon, Jamaica Kincaid, Peter Ackroyd, and Beryl Bainbridge. Under pseudonyms, Cleaver had also written two novels: the mystery *Sherbourne's Folly* under the name Nora Barry, and *Morning Glory* (which became a bestseller in 1984) under the name Julia Cleaver Smith. But when Diane saw the manuscript of *Mama,* she suggested revisions that made Terry suspect that Diane did not really understand the book.

"Eventually," Kessenich continued, "Terry came to me and said she wasn't satisfied with Diane. I think she just thought she wasn't aggressive and committed or intense enough. I mean, she wanted someone with more push.

"Terry had wonderful energy. She was a very warm and positive person. I remember when I first talked to her. She was doing data entry for a law firm in New York, I think it was in Rockefeller Center, and she was actually making more money than I was. We were just talking about work, and it came up in conversation, and I said, 'You make more money than I do!' But she was also apparently phenomenal, because she typed—I don't remember what the rate was, but it was something incredible, like 175 words a minute. Or whatever was the possible range, she was very much at the top of it.

"She was very excited, she was thrilled to have an editor, to have someone to work with on it, she was very willing to work on the novel, and that whole part worked very well.

"I would go down to New York regularly to see agents, so I wanted to take Terry out for lunch. I think it was going to be the first time we met. And I said, 'Well, where would you like to go?' thinking she would pick some relatively modest place. She says, 'How about the Four Seasons? I've always wanted to go to the Four Seasons.' And I said, 'Oh what the heck, I've never done it either!' So we had a hundred-fifty-dollar lunch. She loved it, she seemed perfectly at home there. It wasn't like she was awestruck. She's very determined. I saw that in her. I said, she's gonna be a success one way or another. But I never got the feeling that she would run over people. She just has an internal focus.

"One thing I liked to do at sales conferences was to bring authors in, even if they weren't going to do anything like give a talk to the salespeople (there were usually only one or two authors who did that, and they were usually the real big-time authors, and so that didn't happen with a first novelist). But I liked to bring them in to meet the sales people. I figured if they had an image of the person and met the person and liked the person, they'd be less likely to just skip over their work. And just having talked to Terry on the phone, I knew that she'd handle herself very well—she's a very outgoing, very social person. So I invited her to come up to Boston, and she stayed with my wife and I think my daughter was a year at the time, and I forget how old her son was but he was probably a couple of years older. I couldn't put her up in a hotel, so I invited her to my house. She was very warm, and we were very comfortable having her. It's not unusual for editors and their authors to become friends. I've visited other authors in their homes, I don't think it's that uncommon.

"A sales conference is pretty simple. Different places do it differently, but basically, all the sales people are sitting around at a U-shaped table where they can see each other, and the editors go up one at a time, by category or whatever, and present the books. They basically tell the salespeople what the book is about, what the story is behind it, what are the selling points of it, and why you think this story will sell. That was the formal part of it.

"The sales department also had lots of meetings on its own, where they came up with the original estimates of what they thought they could sell of the book, broken down by geographical areas and things like that. It's where they work out all that stuff, and the editorial and marketing people come and give them a sense of how they should go about selling it. They try to give them selling points, some hints and clues, and try to tell them something about the author, if there's anything interesting about the author that can grab attention. Publicity people are there too. So basically it's planning the strategy. A lot of it's prepared ahead of time to present to them, but that's where it all sort of comes together and you get a sense of what the possibility of the book is.

"The casual part of it is, we go out to dinner. I always emphasize to my authors, unless they bring it up, don't talk to them about selling the book. The point is for them to meet you and like you and so they'll work harder selling the book. And the other thing is you have no money to spend.

"Let me tell you just how hard she worked. I had had another author that I worked with, an author that I also brought to a sales conference. And beyond that, I knew as an editor that unless somebody thinks for some reason a first novel could make it huge, they get no backing. Basically they're put out there, they get into the bookstores, and you hope they get reviewed and people find them and that's really about it for most of them. And I knew that would be the case with this book. So I said, we need to make some kind of personal impression on booksellers. So I'm going to get a list of all the booksellers in the country and we're gonna have you write personal letters to them. I think we made postcards just to make it cheaper, but he actually wrote personal notes on every one of them, to hundreds and hundreds of people. And his novel did slightly better than the average first novel, and so it seemed to have some effect. I think it had a particularly strong effect in his region because the novel had a strong regional quality to it.

"So with that experience in mind, I explained that whole thing to Terry, and she, like most authors, was taken aback. She was a little shocked at how little a publishing house would do for a first novel. So I said, but look, we can do something about this. And I told her that plan, and I also said to her, 'And you've got another advantage: You're a black woman. There just aren't that many black female writers, and those two things have a kind of appeal that I didn't have with this other white male writer.' So we talked about writing to places like black studies programs and women's studies programs. So Terry, with her 175-word-a-minute typing, started cranking out letters. And I do believe she told me she sent out over a thousand letters. She sent them to women's studies programs, black studies programs, public libraries, and I don't remember if we did bookstores. But what happened was, she managed to get so many requests to do reading at various places like public libraries and universities and stuff like that, that we had to set up a tour for her. I mean, she basically created the tour stops for us. And once she'd done that, then I was able to convince the publicity department to get in there and pay for her airfare and her hotel and stuff like that in these various cities. Because she would get two or three readings in every place she went. I can't remember exactly how many cities it was, but it could have been six. It was amazing, it was absolutely amazing. She essentially created her own tour. She just didn't really like the idea that the publishing house doesn't do more, which of course no author ever does. But it wasn't like she was treated any differently than any other first novelist, and once this stuff did start to kick in, her publicist started to work hard for her.

"She was really sort of depressed when I told her the situation with a first novel—when she learned just how little effort was going to be put into promoting it. I think she expected much more. I mean, the only books you know about are the ones that are being promoted. You're not really aware of how many books are out there for which you never see an ad. And I think just because she's an ambitious person, she would think her book would be one of those that would be advertised and get some attention."

As Kessenich described, Terry's excitement about the forthcoming publication of her book had turned to dismay in July 1986, when she learned that the most the company would probably do was send out a press release and photo, together with a copy of the book, to television stations and radio shows, and then wait to hear if someone expressed interest.

And there Terry was, hoping for ads in *The New York Times Book Review,* a twenty-city book tour, a big window display in Fifth Avenue bookstores, and guest appearances on *Good Morning America* and *Oprah.*

"I learned quickly that this is standard operation procedure for most first novels, and even some second novels if the first one wasn't well received," she wrote the following year in a how-to article appearing in the January/February 1988 issue of *Coda,* the magazine of the organization Poets and Writers. "Let me warn you now. Get used to hearing, 'We can't, we wish we could, but we can't.' "

In the piece—which was another way of recycling her experiences into articles—she gave step-by-step instructions to upcoming writers and other first-time novelists, as to exactly how she promoted her book so that it would not be forgotten and remaindered like she had seen happen to so many other authors and first books. "You'll do well to do what I did," she urged. "Take matters into your own hands."

"I'd heard too many horror stories about first novels never being reviewed, never being available in bookstores, and most terrifying of all to me was the thought of being remaindered, reviewers panning my novel and thus, never selling enough copies of my book to see a royalty check. Well, I didn't want to be one of them."

She went on to describe how she went to her reference bookshelf and searched through her books on writing, finally hitting the jackpot with the 1978 book *How to Get Happily Published: A Complete and Candid Guide* by Judith Appelbaum and Nancy Evans. She turned to the chapter called "Why and How to Be Your Own Best Salesman," where the authors seemed to be talking directly to her. "With 39,000 new books each year and scores of periodicals starting up all the time," they confirmed, "only a small percentage of what's published catches the attention of the public. This reality comes as . . . an especially severe shock to authors of first books." Yet, they continued, there was a way to make sure a book didn't "vanish without a trace three months after publication," and proceeded in simple, empathetic, and encouraging language to explain in detail the inner workings of the publishing industry and how authors could create interest in and an audience for their own books. Terry lapped it up and then got to work. It was the beginning of the summer, and all her friends were hanging out on the beach, but Terry had a goal, and decided to sacrifice that summer of fun for a summer of promotion. There would be other summers.

Lucky for her, she was working in the legal profession. State-of-the-art technology that was available to her as an employee was a godsend, a time-saver, and a money-saver. After spending time in the library compiling lists of the target audience she wanted to know about the book (all the black organizations in the country; women's studies programs; all black newspapers, magazines, radio, and TV programs; all the black colleges; and black studies programs), she keyed their names and addresses into the computer and printed out the labels. Then she wrote her cover letters and merged the names and addresses into the letters. Even Solomon, then three years old, helped: She showed him how to use a sponge to seal the flaps of the envelopes and throw them into a Macy's shopping bag for her to mail—from the law firm, courtesy of "the guys in the mailroom." In total she sent out over four thousand letters over a six-month period, and spent about $700. "Most independent book publicists charge about $3,000," she remarked, "and they basically end up doing the same thing that you can do yourself."

In addition to also sending letters to her friends and everyone in her phone book, she also "picked names of authors whom I'd heard of and respected from a listing in *A Directory of American Poets and Fiction Writers* [also published by Poets & Writers]. I ended up with over 450 names. So what if E. L. Doctorow and Ann Beattie had never heard of me? By the time my book came out, they would."

Terry also sent personal notes to all the Houghton sales representatives "telling them that I hoped they liked my book, were excited by it, and how much I appreciated their efforts to do as much as possible to secure a home in as many bookstores as possible for *Mama.*" But just in case the sales reps weren't enthusiastic about the book, she sent more letters to 1,010 bookstores that she had carefully selected from industry directories in the library, letting them know about the book and offering to do readings.

By the end of that summer, she had several invitations for readings. So she scheduled her own book publicity tour and let her publicist know where she was going. The novel received many reviews, most of them positive—and Terry gave thirty-nine readings from San Francisco to Kentucky, Boston, Atlanta, New York, Berkeley, and Philadelphia.

The book's publication date was set for January 15, 1987. But by then, because of her hard work, she had created so much advance interest in the book that the day before the official publication date, *Mama* had sold out of its first printing of 5,000 copies.

Terry's dedication read, "For my own Mama, Madeline Tillman, whose love and support made everything possible." On the acknowledgment page, she thanked Larry Kessenich, "who said yes in the first place and gave me constant pep talks and reassurance."

And then there was that Gerald Stern poem, "When I Have Reached the Point of Suffocation," that Terry used in the beginning of the book.

Gerald Stern was born in Pittsburgh, Pennsylvania, in 1925,

but his first book of poems was not published until he was forty-six. Before becoming well known, he was one of those poets that Terry had not wanted to become, who had to work several jobs to survive. But in 1977, his book *Lucky Life* was published, and he became famous. One reviewer said, "Reading Stern's poetry is like listening to the words of a loving grandparent who has been through his or her share of painful experiences but has come to terms with them through wisdom gained from a long life." Later, Stern would become a distinguished professor of literature, at the University of Iowa, the University of Pittsburgh, Columbia University, New York University, and Princeton University, among others.

By the time Terry selected his poem for her book, Stern had won many awards and fellowships; his other books of poetry published up to that point included *Lovesick* (1987), *Paradise Poems* (1984), *The Red Coal* (1981), and *Rejoicings* (1973), from which she had chosen "When I Have Reached the Point of Suffocation." Interesting how those particular words touched her; placed in the front of her book, they tip us off to the fact that this is going to also be a story about how a writer makes her "own regeneration out of nothing."

Six weeks after its release date, *Mama* was in its third printing. Terry was a guest on seven television shows and six radio shows (some nationally syndicated), was interviewed in over a dozen newspapers, and the book was reviewed in over thirty newspapers. Her book tour included colleges, jazz clubs, community centers, and small black bookstores.

The bottom line was that she had taken the responsibility to make sure it had happened. "All I know," she wrote, "is if I hadn't done it, what would I have to compare it to? It was hard work but it was worth every penny and every minute I spent."

On the day the book came out, Terry took Solomon to the bookstores "to see if they had *Mama* on the shelves—the shocker was that most of them did, and when I told them I was the author all of them asked me to autograph the books!"

Not only had Terry McMillan saved her own first-novel-by-an-unknown-author from obscurity, but, the success of her self-promotion campaign showed publishers that there was a way to sell to black American readers. This audience was more responsive to Terry's grass-roots appearances than to the usual methods used by the publishing companies.

But the other thing that had happened was that Terry was now, if not famous, at least *visible:* She'd exposed herself to the public. And when that happens you have to be ready for it. A strong-willed person, Terry had the constitution, at least. But still, it was hard to make the transition.

"I was surprised at the reaction to my book," she said in 1987. "I had no idea I'd get so many reviews."

One such review in *Library Journal* (one of the important industry magazines, read by librarians to help decide which books to purchase for their collections) said:

Mama, a first novel, tells of a proud black woman, Mildred Peacock, and her five children. After a violent fight, Mildred throws her drunken husband out of the house. On her own in the poor town of Point Haven, Michigan, Mildred scrimps and drinks, works and goes on welfare, struggling to raise her kids and keep her sanity. Mildred's closest bond is to her oldest daughter, Freda, and their lives parallel each other's progress from despair to hope. The book's main weakness is that the author apparently could not decide what to leave out. She also has not decided who her audience is: At times she seems to be writing to blacks, at other times to be explaining things to naive white readers. Although the story has power, it lacks focus and a clear point of view.

To those who felt the book was one hundred percent autobiographical, Terry retorted, "Some events in the book really happened. There are the same number of children in my family, I moved to California when I was seventeen, my mother and my two sisters came, my brother has been to prison, he did use dope at one point. I used to drink. But I don't drink any more, and I depict Freda as this lush. My brother asked me if I had ever been raped and the answer is no. One of my aunts thinks she's in the book and is not speaking to me. My mother is not an alcoholic. What I did was take my experience and exaggerate it. Everybody's work is autobiographical, despite what they say."

Some saw *Mama* as an unflattering portrayal of black people. Terry was ready for them too. "This book is not mean to represent or portray any gender or group of people," she remarked. "Nobody thinks that a Czech writer is representing all Czechs, or a Russian writer is writing for all Russians."

One reader who was not offended was Terry's real mama—on whom the book was based, after all, and who was quite proud of Terry. "She said she laughed hard and cried hard," Terry related for her hometown newspaper. "She said it brought back a lot of memories, and she's glad to have them in black and white, so that she can really remember."

Terry easily earned out her advance, and the royalty checks were coming in every few months: Finally, she was actually earning money from her writing. But it was not a truly steady income—it wasn't as if she could retire. And so she continued writing.

Yet, the book took on a life of its own. A year after its publication, Houghton circulated the galleys to paperback publishing houses who were invited to make an offer to publish the paperback edition. A company called Washington Square Press (a division of Simon & Schuster) bought the rights to publish it in paperback.

By then, she had a new agent, courtesy of Larry Kessenich.

"Terry had come to me and asked for recommendations of other agents," Kessenich explains, "and I recommended several agents. Molly Friedrich was one of them. I knew Molly very well. She was one of the first two agents that I'd gotten to know. Molly's an incredibly straightforward person, gives you the straight goods on anything, and is not hesitant to do it, but is not unkind or anything like that. I had a sense that Molly would probably be the person that she'd want; Molly had the energy and focus that Terry was looking for."

D. T. Max was the editor at Washington Square Press who acquired the paperback rights to *Mama.*

Max remembers offering Houghton Mifflin about $7,500 for the paperback rights, which the publisher accepted. "Then her agent, Molly Friedrich, who I think knew what a big deal she had coming, said No, that's not enough. We wound up paying a very small additional sum above that. It was far below what she would have been worth a month or two later, for that matter.

"We had published the paperback versions of Alice Walker's *The Color Purple* and Toni Morrison's *The Bluest Eye,* so we were alert to the sales potential of African American women's fiction particularly, and I was in effect on the lookout for appropriate books. Editors look at what other similar books have done. And it was clear that there was a great interest in black women's writing. *The Color Purple* had been a huge best-seller two years before, one of the biggest books of the decade. I was getting all these letters addressed to Alice Walker, but they were from all over the country. They were letters from real people, and especially from real black people, and I thought, There's a huge market, a huge world out here that she's going to reach that Terry could reach too.

"Terry caught a number of trends. One was the incredible number of women who were buying trade paperback books. Another trend was that the education level of African Americans was rising, and also the leisure income. So she was able to be present at just the moment when a big black marketplace was growing, which I don't think had existed ten years before.

"I met her for lunch at a sushi restaurant after we bought the rights to the book. And I could immediately tell that she was somebody who had a huge amount of energy for presenting herself as aggressively as possible and making herself well known. At the time, she was working as a typist at night, or word processor. And she had obviously organized all these people among the word processors to come out and support her book, and she had sent out on the office word processing equipment hundreds or thousands, I don't remember which, of press releases to various organizations. Many people asked, Well why don't we do that for our own books? I said, Well you have to have Terry's personality to pull it off—it's not easy.

"She was proud of the book, but she wasn't particularly focused on it on a sentence-by-sentence basis. She was more interested in who it had reached and who would care about it, and whose life it portrayed."

But as tempting as it may have been, Terry wasn't sitting around resting on her laurels, waiting for the royalty checks to come in.

5

Go West, Young Black Woman

It takes spunk . . . to get out of the ethnic cocoon.
—Ishmael Reed

By the spring of 1987 Terry was embarking on another serendipitous adventure, courtesy of Ishmael Reed. The year before, Reed—who has a lot of support among academics all over the world and gets to go everywhere—had done a reading of his poetry at the University of Wyoming in Laramie, of all places.

"I knew I'd finally get to Laramie because every other movie I saw when I was a kid took place in either Cheyenne or Laramie," jokes Reed. "Laramie's like an old cowboy town. It hasn't changed very much since the nineteenth century. They have these pony express stops and everything. It's the West.

"They told me that they were looking for a teacher who would be willing to come to Wyoming, which was a godforsaken place. And I remember that Terry was really struggling with some kinda job. I knew she had never taught before. She was a single mother and everything, and she would often call me for advice. When I heard this job was available, I called her immediately."

It didn't matter to Reed that Terry had never taught before.

"I knew by the manuscripts she was sending me that she was ready. She knew her way around. I mean, Terry's very forceful and she's very articulate. I figured that after all these years of writing and attending these workshops and everything, she could teach a course in writing. She knew the strategies and the mechanics of it. So I told them that I had a perfect candidate. And she went out there to teach.

"Most people would probably want to stay in New York. This was a great introduction for her to the West. There are very few black people there. It takes spunk to do that, to get out of the ethnic cocoon, to go to places like that. She always had spunk. You go to some of these western towns and you're the only black person there. I remember when I got stuck in North Platte, Nebraska, and the whole town wanted to take care of me. So I mean, there are still some surprises in the United States. She went to Laramie and those people fell in love with her. She was a good teacher and they wanted to keep her. I heard from them, and they were very satisfied with her. They wanted her to stay there, and they wanted to give her tenure. I think that was a terrific experience for her."

"We hired her at the time *Mama* came out. It was a huge success," says Lisa Shipley, assistant to the head of the English department at the University of Wyoming at Laramie. "We thought we'd pulled a coup.

"Our department is one of the largest departments on campus. I imagine that at that time we had twenty-eight or twenty-nine tenure track faculty members. We're a little smaller than that now. We had lecturers also, part-time people. They taught full time but were considered part time because their positions didn't necessarily continue. They were generally one-year appointments. Terry's was a temporary one-year appointment. John Wideman had left us the year before. We often get visiting professors when someone retires or resigns as a way of meeting student demand while we are searching for a permanent replacement.

"[The requirements are] based more on record than on education. If you were looking for someone to teach Shakespeare, you would look for more education than research or publication. But with creative writing we look more for the record, that is, your publications.

"I liked Terry right off. She was outgoing and charismatic. Terry was well liked, and we were well satisfied with her and her performance here."

"I knew I wanted to leave Brooklyn—but Wyoming?" Terry wrote to the "Letters from Home" section of *Wigwag* magazine. "Anyway, when I got the call offering me a position at the University of Wyoming and a paid invitation to come out and 'have a look,' I said, 'what the hell,' and went."

Wyoming is in the western United States, where the flat middle section of the country, the Great Plains, finally bumps up against the Rocky Mountains. The city of Laramie, in the western section of the state, is 7,165 feet above sea level. As Terry related the story for *Wigwag,* she arrived in Denver on April 11, and was picked up by Keith Hull, the acting chairman of the English department, and his sixteen-year-old daughter, for the two-hour drive to Laramie. That day, the drive took four hours because of a raging snowstorm they encountered.

On this fact-finding trip, Terry wrote, she quickly got a feel for the little university town. For example, its tiny population of not quite 35,000—which dropped by ten thousand in the summer when the university students were all gone. It sure wasn't Brooklyn—in fact, it was more like Port Huron.

She described the downtown area, which was maybe two blocks long.

"I felt like I'd been thrown back in time about forty years," she wrote. "All the little stores looked hopeless, as if they were begging for business. There was one shoe store, and a J. C. Penney whose mannequins still wore their hair in starched pageboys and whose hands reached out for something that wasn't there. Sears was just a counter where you could order things from the catalog."

Back in Brooklyn, after giving it a lot of thought, Terry decided, What the hell. She began packing, gave away all her furniture, and sent a deposit for rental of a town house—based only on a written description. In June, Terry, this time with three-year-old Solomon, got off the plane again in Denver to drive to Laramie, her home for the next year. Or to be more precise, a 2,100-square-foot, three-bedroom, two-bathroom duplex featuring a huge family room with a wood-burning stove, a utility room, a living room with a working fireplace, a dining room, a kitchen with garbage disposal and dishwasher, a back deck, a garage, and a 180-degree view of the mountains of the Medicine Bow National Forest.

All of that real estate cost Terry $515 a month.

It was truly a new experience for her. First, although the town may have looked ordinary, there was one important topographical factor: It was over seven thousand feet above sea level. That is significant altitude, and it takes a while for the human body to accustom itself to altitude. At first you feel nothing, so you run, or walk fast, or climb stairs, just like you normally would. Then suddenly there's a burning and aching in your chest, and you learn where your lungs are, because that's them hurting you. Then you understand the comments that you had previously ignored when you arrived: "It'll take a few weeks to get used to the altitude."

Second, because altitude means you're closer to the sun and the air is thinner, you get a tan, even in the winter.

Third, Laramie is in the Mountain time zone. This time zone is one hour ahead of California, where Terry's family lived, and two hours behind New York, where her friends lived. She was away from her mom, who stayed behind in Los Angeles, although they spoke often by phone.

Terry's neighbors were all white, but they were nice—especially when they learned she was teaching at the university—and had kids that Solomon could play with. Solomon loved the space, the mountains, and the sunshine. She heard that there were sixty-two other black people in town, but she never saw that many.

"There were only fourteen kids at Solomon's preschool," she wrote, "but they had three teachers and 8,000 square feet of playground with real equipment. Every Monday they got swimming lessons; Wednesdays they went roller-skating, and Thursdays they'd go on field trips. Solomon was three and a half and could say his numbers and colors in Spanish. It cost me under $150 a month for this. I was starting to like it here."

One of the hardest things Terry had to do was change her shopping habits—it was Kmart, not Bloomie's, that was the local hot store. Her family teased her unmercifully for shopping at Big K. In New York, she could get her groceries daily, because there were butchers, fruit and vegetable markets, and fish markets within a stone's throw of her apartment. In Laramie, she had to buy groceries to last a week or two because the local supermarket was so far away.

There were no beaches in Wyoming like there were in California, although there were lakes up in the nearby mountains. And there wasn't much in the way of cultural activity. On special occasions there would be a rodeo, maybe a carnival. For entertainment, Terry went to the movies or watched videos. In the winter, she went skiing twice a week.

Still, over the summer, she began to relax, started to get comfortable. She had time to read and to write, and she felt like a real person. When people asked her if living there was a culture shock, she told them that it wasn't, because it just reminded her of her Michigan hometown.

Good things were happening every day. One day she just happened to be passing by a car dealer's lot, and a red 1987 Toyota Celica five-speed with a sunroof just happened to catch her eye. The saleswoman just happened to chat her up, and within a few minutes had turned Terry's protests about not being in a position to buy a new car and not having the best credit rating into "Of course you are. Do you know how many professors we get in here whose credit is shit? First thing Monday morning I'll have an answer for you." On Monday morning Terry picked up the car.

As for her own writing, the connections and contacts she had made, the visibility she had, were all seeds she had sown, and they were bearing fruit. She had already racked up some awards for her work: a 1986 New York Foundation for the Arts fellowship, and the Doubleday/Columbia University Literary fellowship. She contributed pieces to the *New York Times Magazine's* "Hers" column, and got assignments to review books for the *Atlanta Constitution*, the *Philadelphia Inquirer*, and *The New York Times Book Review*. She also began working on her second novel, *A Day Late and a Dollar Short*, which she had started before *Mama* had been published. It revisited her theme of a black mother—also greatly inspired by Terry's mother Madeline—named Viola Price. In the story Viola laments, in cutting, no-holds-barred language, that none of her four grown kids turned out the way she wanted them. "Sometimes I can't believe they all came out of my body, grew up in the same house," Viola laments. "The truth is, I love them like they just got here, but I'm tired of mothering them."

Terry enjoyed teaching. And again, serendipity struck: The teaching position, which she had gotten by accident, led her to another writing project, which she did out of necessity.

Part of her aim for the fiction workshop she taught was to introduce her students to good contemporary fiction writers, and she took special care to find material for her class to read. Looking through many anthologies of short stories, she came to a startling realization: "It just hit me, there are no black writers, no Third World writers" represented in those anthologies, she said, despite the fact that she could think of a few dozen such writers. While she knew such contemporary black writers existed, there was no anthology of their writing. She was already up to date on every annual anthology of contemporary writers, including *Pushcart, Editor's Choice, Prize Stories: The O. Henry Awards,* and *The Best American Short Stories,* and black quarterlies such as *Callaloo, Catalyst, Sage,* and *Hambone.* After doing some research, she wrote a proposal for a book that would compile the writings of contemporary black writers.

Trying to come up with a name for such a collection, she writes in the introduction to it, "I was looking out my window at the snow piled up, the thick icicles hanging off the house, and I thought about how . . . as African American writers we have . . . been breaking ice not only in getting published, but [in] getting the respect and attention our work deserves." She named the collection *Breaking Ice.*

She approached ninety writers for material for the anthology; among the final choices were Tina McElroy Ansa, Doris Jean Austin, Arthur Flowers, Bill Williams Forde, Darryl Pinckney,

Ishmael Reed, Barbara Summers, and fifty others, both established and emerging. John Edgar Wideman, her predecessor at the University of Wyoming at Laramie, wrote the preface. Terry's contribution, "Ma'Dear," was about a seventy-two-year old widow who misses her man.

Which is in a way what Terry was going through. Although lots of young white boys were after her, there was nothing happening on the love life front. One of her ex-boyfriends even called her to gloat, saying "It's lonely at the top, isn't it, baby?"

The fall of 1987 also brought some sad news from the black literary world: Two of Terry's inspirations passed away. On October 27, John Oliver Killens, one of the founders of the Harlem Writers Guild, died in New York City of cancer at the age of seventy-one. And thousands of miles across the Atlantic, in St.-Paul-de-Vence, France, James Baldwin closed his eyes for the last time, on November 30.

After spending a year in Wyoming, cabin fever plus Terry's natural wanderlust kicked in. Terry was feeling that familiar urge to move on. Small things began to irritate her, and the place gave her that Port Huron feeling: boring.

By the time the snow and below-freezing temperatures arrived that winter of 1987, she was well ready to break out of Laramie, but wasn't sure how. Then, in late December, both she and Solomon were laid up with a virus, and there was nothing to do but look out the window at the results of a three-day snowfall. Terry, bored out of her mind, was happy just to hear the ringing telephone—and even happier to learn that the call was from the University of Arizona, wanting to know if Terry might be interested in a position at the school. Her first question was not about the salary. She wrote:

" 'How cold is it now?' I asked.

" 'Seventy-five.'

"I looked at the frost on the windows, at my $281 heating bill, and said yes."

And so she was led on another adventure. On May 24, 1988, she sent an announcement to her friends to let them know that she and Solomon would be leaving the cold prairie for the hot desert, as of June 1. The University of Arizona in Tucson was getting Terry McMillan as an associate professor of creative writing.

6

Disappearing Acts

*I'm sorry I did not make Zora barefoot, pregnant, getting her
ass kicked in the projects. But that's not the story I wanted
to tell. I cannot apologize because some of us have been
to college, okay?*

—Terry McMillan

It was summer 1988, and once again, Terry and Solomon had
relocated. They were in another beautiful place. Red earth.
Palm trees. No snow. Terry kept in touch with Leonard—although sporadically—by mail and phone, but Leonard and Solomon did not see each other that often.

Tucson, Arizona—two states south of Wyoming—was a city
surrounded by mountains. Evidence of its rich cultural heritage—Spanish, Mexican, and Native American—was everywhere: adobe homes, mariachi bands, rodeos, country music,
and a few skyscrapers too. There were canyons and prehistoric
Indian ruins. To the west, there was Las Vegas, San Diego, and
the Baja Peninsula. The Grand Canyon was 341 miles away, and
Santa Fe, 501 miles away.

The first black Tucson settlers were Mr. and Mrs. Wiley Box, a couple who arrived from Oklahoma between 1850 and 1855. Later black Tucsonites included farmers, miners, prospectors, cowboys, buffalo soldiers (the Ninth and Tenth Cavalry and the 24th and 25th Infantry Regiments), cooks, barbers, and maids. By 1933, there were a number of black businesses, among them restaurants, shoe shine parlors, service stations, and car repair shops, with names like Peggy Watson's Chat and Chew Cafe, Jimmy's Chicken Shack, and Tommy Scott Cleaners. Local blacks were kept informed of relevant news by way of the newspaper *Arizona's Negro Journal*.

In those days, racial discrimination and segregation were a way of life in Tucson. Blacks could not eat at the dime store lunch counter, and black children could not swim in the city's pool unless it was the last day of the week—the day before they drained the water. Audiences in movie theaters were segregated: In 1942, one theater made headlines in the black press for refusing to seat black soldiers. Even important black visitors to Tucson were treated this way: Black baseball players on the Cleveland Indians team had trouble finding places to stay and eat during spring training, and when Marian Anderson, the famous contralto, came to Tucson in 1942, no hotel would accommodate her. Until the 1960s, blacks were prevented from owning or renting property in many areas of Tucson. As a result, they established their own neighborhoods, one of which was along a street called South Park Avenue.

....

But Terry wanted to make some black history of her own—in her bedroom. Problem was, there was just no action man-wise.

Tucson, to Terry, was just another small town, like Laramie, like Port Huron. And although the population was 600,000, blacks comprised only 3 percent of that population. She soon made friends, most of whom were married but a few of whom were single, and they kept their eyes open to find poor Terry a little somethin' somethin'. In an essay that appeared in the November 1989 issue of *Wigwag*, Terry wrote about the problems she had trying to meet men, and when she did, trying to have relationships with them. In fact, that was becoming a recurring theme in all the articles she wrote.

In the article, she described how her buddies did their part to hook her up. First, they let her know about all the places she could go to dance and hear live music. (Tucson had a lot of resort properties, and there were clubs in or near these resorts.) Soon after her arrival, she went to one of these clubs with her married girlfriends, but there was only one black guy there— and he ignored them.

Then, another of her married friends set Terry up with a handsome, college-educated man. She noticed, but tried to ignore, that he was a frequent drinker and a pot smoker. Nevertheless—and using the bird-in-the-hand theory—Terry decided to date him. On their first date, they ran into some friends of his. When he left for the men's room, they expressed to Terry how glad they were that he'd kicked his drug problem—and that he'd told them that he was in love with her. Ignoring all these signals, she went to a hotel room with him. But poor Terry was sadly disappointed at his performance, and ended up having to kick him to the curb. Couldn't even make the reserve squad, this guy.

But her friends, ever hopeful, continued to introduce her to what were considered the best catches in Tucson. Two such guys were forty years old. "One had just lost his job and was living with his mother," Terry wrote in her *Wigwag* piece. "The other drove a Mercedes and sold real estate. He stopped calling when he found out I'd bought a house through another agent."

Her mother, who would soon come to live in Tucson herself, gave Terry advice by telephone:

"Get out more. No one's gonna walk up and ring your doorbell. Make yourself visible.

"Keep looking.

"You need to leave Solomon at home more. Any man in his right mind would swear you're married, because you take him everywhere. Get a baby-sitter."

Even Terry's bank teller, a twenty-four-year-old black man, tried to get with her, but she wasn't into younger guys. Or was she? "I'm wondering," she wrote, "if twenty-four really is too young. He's in college. He's got a steady job and abhors drugs. 'I'm almost old enough to be your mother,' I've said to him. 'So what?' he says."

At least Terry was living in another fabulous house. Once again, she had been led to it. Earning good money now, she discovered that she needed a tax shelter, "and in America that means property." After a few months of collecting brochures, making lists of requirements, visiting countless models, and even impulsively making a few down payments on houses she liked (and of which she requested refunds later), she found it. It was in a new development called Copper Creek, in an award-winning school district, near a country club and golf course. The house was 2,300 square feet, with lots of windows, three bedrooms, a family room, sixteen-foot ceilings, a breathtaking view of the mountains, "and a staircase so high and wide that when I sat on the top step I felt like Scarlett O'Hara." The cost, with all the optional extras: $136,910.

Her kind and helpful neighbors—all white except for one family two doors down—"found it hard to believe that a single black woman could come up with 'all this money' for such a 'luxury' house. 'How'd you ever manage?' one asked, while another exclaimed, 'Gee, you're so brave!' "

In one of the "Hers" articles that she wrote for *The New York Times,* Terry candidly expressed the requirements for her ideal man. She dreamed that he would be "a black man who feels good enough about himself so that he's not threatened by me. That he's not out to control or mold me. . . . In the dream, he laughs a lot. In the dream he's smart. In the dream he loves children. In the dream he's physical. In the dream we love each other, treat each other with kindness and respect."

Most likely, she was imagining this fantasy man because of her failed relationship with Leonard Welch. But even that failure was reinventing itself, into inspiration for another story—a story set in Brooklyn, New York, about a turbulent relationship between one Zora Banks, a middle-class black woman aspiring to be a songwriter (and so named in honor of Zora Neale Hurston), and one Franklin Swift, a high school dropout and frequently unemployed building contractor with a drug problem. Franklin's frustration causes extreme problems in the relationship. Each chapter alternates between Franklin's voice and Zora's voice, providing each person's view of the relationship.

"I was trying to understand what happened in my relationship," Terry later explained in an interview. "I fell in love with a man who was not as educated as I am. The problems in the relationship come from the bad decisions this man made because of his hang-ups. I wanted to put myself in this man's shoes, to see his side of the story. In every relationship there are two sides to every story. When you're honest you don't have anything to lose."

She submitted a portion of the manuscript of this story, which she called *Disappearing Acts,* to Houghton Mifflin, as her contract for *Mama* had given them an option on her second novel. Larry Kessenich describes how the company lost out on publishing it:

"With the second novel, they wanted $20,000 on the basis of a partial manuscript, the first hundred or so pages. And frankly, I just wasn't that confident about it. I didn't think it was as strong as *Mama,* I didn't think it had the intensity of *Mama.*

"That really upset Terry. She felt that I wasn't showing confidence in her. And I suppose you could say that was true. But Houghton Mifflin was very conservative, and you just didn't take things on the basis of somebody's name; you had to feel like you had some substance there. The first novel, as I said, did slightly better than the average first novel, but not so much so that you'd have any kind of certainty what would happen with the second one. And I just didn't feel like we had enough of a sense of how the second one would do to warrant that kind of advance, which was at least four or perhaps five times more than what she got with *Mama*.

"I didn't feel like the content was hopeless. I just felt like I needed to see what the novel was going to be like. I'd seen many novels, even ones that started out really well, that fell apart in the second half. And I had some doubts even about how this one had started out. It wasn't that I was saying definitely no, I was just saying 'I need to see the rest of the novel.' But she wanted to sell it on the basis of the first novel. Which—at that time, anyway—was pretty unusual for a second novel by an author who hadn't sold phenomenally well. Sure, if you had somebody who came along and their first novel sold thirty, forty thousand copies, you might be willing to take a chance on the second one, on a partial manuscript. But as I said, we'd had to do a fair amount of work on the first novel. There's also such a thing as one-novel authors. So all those things entered in. I'd gotten the advice of other people, and our feeling was just very simply, we want to see a complete novel. And it wasn't even that we wouldn't have considered that amount of money, having seen the rest of it. But she had no patience, she felt that I was saying I didn't have confidence in her ability to write a second novel. So they took it elsewhere and they got what they wanted.

"In hindsight, I think I didn't understand just how powerful her ability to promote herself was and how that was likely to lead to success for her. But I'm just not sure that Houghton could ever do for her what she wanted. Whoever took her on, there had to be a sense that they had someone they could really build, make into a big author. To be perfectly honest I don't think we did have that sense at Houghton Mifflin. We thought it might be the kind of slow climb kind of thing that happens, but I don't think anybody had a sense we could break her out with a second book.

"In a way Molly was apologetic, but not really. She knew she had to do what her author wanted, and she believed pretty strongly in Terry and I think that she maybe had a better sense than I did of where she could go. There was no rancor there. I felt bad that they were going to go somewhere else and that we weren't going to get a chance to even consider the second novel as a complete novel, but people gotta do what they gotta do. I knew enough about the plight of authors. If they feel like they're not supported, they have to go somewhere where they can get a better deal. Publishing houses are perfectly willing to let *them* go, so there's no reason why they shouldn't be willing to let the publishing house go."

Terry has explained that another reason she took the manuscript elsewhere was that Houghton wanted her to drop Zora's voice because Zora, being middle class and all, sounded too much like a white girl. "They weren't acknowledging that we had other experiences," she said in an interview. "Because this woman is educated, because her mother left her an inheritance, therefore she sounds white? Everything was supposed to be racially motivated. We don't just fall in love and get our hearts broken just like everybody else. No, there's got to be something about being exploited. I'm sorry I did not make Zora barefoot, pregnant, getting her ass kicked in the projects. But that's not the story I wanted to tell. I cannot apologize because some of us have been to college, okay?"

Terry also complained that the Houghton editors "were so impressed with Franklin's voice and the fact that I was pulling it off that they wanted me to write the whole book from his point of view. It was going to be this coup: black woman writes story from black man's point of view, it's never been done, blah, blah, blah blah, blah blah. Well, I didn't write *Disappearing Acts* to prove anything; that was the way the story had to be told."

After the Houghton situation fell through, Molly Friedrich promptly sent the chapters to Viking Penguin. It took Penguin only two days to purchase the manuscript.

Penguin published *Disappearing Acts* in August 1989. Terry's dedication was "For Solomon, years from now." On August 11, Terry sent a copy of the book to his daddy, Leonard, with a one-page typewritten letter. In it, she proudly presented the book, emphasizing to Leonard that it was a love story and quoting *The New York Times* review, which had called it that too. She further cautioned him:

"Don't read this like it's YOUR biography or YOUR story." In her strong, steady handwriting, inside the copy of the book she sent Leonard Terry wrote a loving inscription—but again advised him to ". . . try to read it as *fiction,* because I took liberties in order to make the story more plausible."

As he read the book, at first Leonard must have felt flattered. The character of Franklin Swift was just like himself: same complexion, same height. Same weight, same hair and mustache. Same age and marital status—even married at the same age. And plenty of other details that were lifted from Leonard's traits and habits: a trick knee, a habit of drip-drying after a shower, working out at the gym, even his preferred breakfast food—all the same as Welch.

Welch read on, seeing similarities everywhere. The character Franklin, just like Welch, was a construction worker who was a carpenter on the side. Franklin too had dropped out of high school after the eleventh grade, and had later gotten his high school equivalency diploma. The character Franklin first met his girlfriend Zora the same way Welch had met Terry. The characters' first argument, over a revealing bathing suit Zora wore, was the same as Leonard and Terry's first argument. Other arguments were similar too. The characters moved to an apartment in a brownstone on Boerum Hill, where the landlord, who owned cats, was named Sol. A trip Leonard and Terry had made to Saratoga Springs, New York, for the Newport Jazz Festival was nearly identical to one the characters took. People who knew Leonard would probably recognize that Franklin was based on him.

But then the character Franklin Swift got uglier. He turned out to be an alcoholic who drank on the job, and hated white people, and was homophobic. He was a rapist who forced himself on his woman. He was hostile, lazy, and used drugs. He was a slacker who was unwilling to work and was content to live off of his woman.

Leonard Welch was not amused.

....

Disappearing Acts went on to sell several hundred thousand copies, making Terry McMillan a familiar name among black readers. In turn, Hollywood became interested, and MGM bought the movie rights to the book and hired Terry to write the screenplay. This project, though, would be delayed for years as other events intervened.

Terry, in her own modest way, was pretty surprised that she was getting all this attention; after all, all she had done was write a story. But she still was glad for the success.

Reader reaction to *Disappearing Acts* ran the gamut: Some were glad Zora didn't give up on Franklin just because he wasn't a college graduate or business executive. That, after all, didn't automatically mean that a man is a low-life good-for-nothing bum. Others saw it as a story of a black man getting a hurt ego because his woman makes more than him. Most readers loved the way that Terry let each character tell his and her side of the story instead of fusing both together from one point of view. Many recognized this kind of relationship as quite familiar; some were disappointed that Terry chose to keep them together after he had raped her, and couldn't understand how he was now worthy of trust. Some didn't like Franklin, because he was crude, disrespectful, and lazy, and felt that Zora should have thrown him out for good.

When Terry met her fans during her appearances, she learned a lot about what effect the book had on them. Some of the copies she autographed had coffee stains, chicken grease, everything, and the owner of that copy would tell how she'd been forced to pass it around to everyone at work. There would be accounts of how someone would spot a co-worker, supposed to be working, laughing her ass off. Questioned, they would be told, "You gotta buy this book." And after a peek, they went out to buy their own copy. Women fans would speak testimonials to Terry's accuracy all the time:

"Terry, girl, I just know you had a movie camera on me for the past two years, 'cause you know *all* my business!"

"Girlfriend, you been sneakin' in my house and checkin' me out?"

"Were we married to the same man?"

"Child, my sex life perked up after I read *Disappearing Acts.*"

And the brothers would say things like:

"I felt better about myself. Thank you for writing this."

The biggest response from the critics was about the profanity in *Disappearing Acts*. After reading one such review which suggested that there was profanity on practically every page, with typical indignance, Terry called her editor.

"I said to [her] when I read that review, 'You know, it's *not* on every fucking page!' then I picked up the galley when I was on the airplane coming to New York, and [when I got there I called her back] and said, 'You know, I think they're right: It *is* on every fucking page!' But so what? That's the way we talk."

7

Waiting to Exhale

I'm glad she got out of New York. Otherwise we wouldn't have gotten Arizona as a setting for a novel written by an African American. (You know our stuff is always in this urban setting.)

—Ishmael Reed

In December 1989, Terry wrote the following for *Wigwag's* "Letter from Home" column:

> One evening I stood in my big bathroom off my master bedroom, trying to figure out which sink to use to wash my face, since one is supposed to be for my husband, which I don't have. The moon was out, so I sat on the deck off the sitting room in my master bedroom and looked up at the stars. "Have I arrived?" I asked the moon. "I mean, is this all there is?"

Miss Terry was lonely and frustrated and whining (although—ever enterprising—she whined on paper—at least she was able to make it pay off!). In the February 1990 issue of *Essence* she once again recycled the subject in an article called "Looking for Mr. Right:"

> I haven't had a steady man in my life for so long that I'm beginning to wonder if I'll ever find one. I keep asking myself, What am I doing wrong? I've done what I consider to be all the right things: I still look good, I'm honest, and I have a lot to offer someone. So why over the last few years have I had only two powerful but short-lived relationships, in which both men just stopped calling one day with no explanation? Sometimes I think that even though a lot of professional men claim to want a smart, independent woman, they're kidding themselves.

What Terry was expressing was nothing new. Whenever women—black, white, anycolor, and everycolor, of every socioeconomic background and culture—get together, this subject invariably comes up. Some of us obsess about the basics of it: Where are they, what do we need to do to connect with them, how do we keep them. Others study it academically, or invent (or patronize) ways of paying for it (personal ads, dating services). The topic has endless subtopics, and plenty of people with opinions and advice. Plenty of books are written about it.

Books? You better believe it. Terry took her lament and began transforming it into a story.

In 1990, Terry's mother Madeline also moved to Tucson from Los Angeles. She loved the desert, and was able to breathe easier there, having developed asthma, a chronic respiratory disease that inflames and swells the mucous lining of the bronchial passages, causing obstruction of breathing. Asthma, which comes from the Greek *asthma,* meaning "panting," affects nearly fifteen million Americans.

Although asthma symptoms differ in each individual, an asthma attack takes place when the lung's bronchial tubes become hypersensitive to a trigger or allergen like dust, pollen, or smoke. The body's immune system reacts by releasing chemicals into the airways, which cause the air passages to swell and fill with thick, mucus. This leaves the asthma sufferer coughing, wheezing, and gasping for air. Some people may only experience a dry coughing spell. Often, asthma attacks take place at night and last for a few hours.

Doctors say that the causes of asthma attacks are complex, and include such things as environmental pollution, cigarette smoke, animal dander, mold, cockroaches, dust mites, and stress.

According to the American Lung Association, black people are three times as likely to be hospitalized for asthma as whites, and four times more likely to be rushed to the emergency room for care related to an asthma attack.

Madeline's condition may have been caused, or exacerbated, by the Los Angeles air quality (or lack thereof). Madeline, not as restless as Terry, joined Mt. Calvary Baptist Church, the oldest black church in Tucson. There was plenty for her to get involved in, as the church had a day care center, music department (including several choirs and an all-male group accompanied by a guitarist, bassist, drummer, pianist, and organist), layman's group, prison ministry, and evangelistic courses. But Madeline's favorite was the Haven of Hope program, which helped children learn to read. It was this program to which Madeline offered her volunteer services.

But ever restless, Madeline's daughter was not so easily pleased or excited by the local social scene. By August 1990, true to her own pattern, she was bored silly with Arizona, and again appealed to Ishmael Reed for help, sending him a copy of her résumé and admitting that she wanted to come back to northern California.

In the fall, Terry was asked to be on the nominating panel that selected the winner of the 1990 National Book Award for fiction. Her fellow panelists were Paul West, William Gass, Philip Lopate, and Catharine Stimpson, the chair.

The five were gathered together in a ritual that had been going on since March 16, 1950. On that day, a consortium of book publishing groups had sponsored the first annual National Book Awards Ceremony and Dinner at the Waldorf-Astoria Hotel in New York City. Their goal was to enhance the public's awareness of exceptional books written by fellow Americans, and to increase the popularity of reading in general.

Since then, every November the prestigious National Book Awards, sponsored by the nonprofit National Book Foundation, are presented to "recognize books of exceptional merit written by Americans" in the categories of Poetry, Fiction, Nonfiction, and Young People's Literature. The winners, selected by five-member, independent judging panels for each genre, each receive a $10,000 cash award and a crystal sculpture. Some consider the National Book Awards to be the Oscars of the book publishing industry.

Between July and August, the five judges begin receiving the books, which may be sent by the publisher only. The judges must spend their summer and part of the fall reading and must narrow down the submissions to a shortlist of the five finalists by sometime in October.

Paul West, then in his midsixties, was an award-winning British author of imaginative novels with titles like *Rat Man of Paris, Lord Byron's Doctor, The Place in Flowers Where Pollen Rests, The Tent of Orange Mist,* and such nonfiction works as *A Stroke of Genius* and *Words for a Deaf Daughter.* His reviews also appeared in the pages of the *New York Times* and *Washington Post.* Critics said that he had an "often acid pen," that "he is as unstinting in his praise of what he admires as he is devastating in his criticism of pretense and ineptitude," and that he possessed "splendid command of the language, shrewd sensibility, and probing intellect."

Then there was William H. Gass, at the time a sixty-six-year-old respected academic and popular teacher who was born in Fargo, North Dakota. Gass received a doctorate in philosophy from Cornell University in 1954, and since his first novel, *Omensetter's Luck* (1966), had been considered one of the most critically acclaimed authors of fiction and criticism. Gass himself won the 1985 National Book Award for a previous essay collection, *Habitations of the Word.*

Catharine Stimpson, the then fifty-four-year-old chair of the committee, was a lesbian and a feminist who had been a radical activist in the sixties. Stimpson, who grew up in a small town in Washington state, had been an English professor at Barnard College, then at Rutgers University until she became dean of the Rutgers graduate school in the mid-1980s. In her own writing, she had compared the plight of women in America to that of blacks, because "What the economy gives both women and blacks are menial labor, low pay, and few promotions." She added that "Blacks and women also live in the wasteland of American sexuality" because "white men, convinced of the holy primacy of sperm . . . have made their sex a claim to power and then used their power to claim control of sex. In fact and fantasy, they have violently segregated black men and white women." Her only novel, *Class Notes* (1979), described a woman much like herself who escapes a string of abusive men by enrolling at an Eastern women's college where she learns the delights of lesbian love. Stimpson once expressed her dream of "a multiracial, multicultural, multispecied world."

Philip Lopate, then a forty-seven-year-old poet, essayist, and novelist, had received his bachelor's degree from Columbia University in 1964, and began writing poems and novels in 1960. From 1968 to 1980, in the New York City public school system, he taught street-wise black and Hispanic children to write poems. He later wrote accounts of his teaching experiences.

So Terry was the youngest and only black member of the National Book Award fiction panel. Terry and the panel selected the fiction finalists from 375 submissions sent by seventy-two publishers. The five books that the panelists chose as finalists were *Chromos* by Felipe Alfau (Dalkey Archive Press), *Paradise* by Elena Castedo (Grove Weidenfeld), *Dogeaters* by Jessica Hagedorn (Pantheon) *Middle Passage* by Charles Johnson (Atheneum), and *Because It Is Bitter, and Because It Is My Heart* by Joyce Carol Oates (E. P Dutton/William Abrahams).

But it seemed as if every year there was some conflict surrounding the National Book Awards. Until 1988, three people had made up the panel of National Book Award fiction and nonfiction judges. That year, the board of directors had decided to increase the panel to five.

In 1987, forty-eight black writers and critics had signed a statement which appeared in *The New York Times Book Review*, expressing their disappointment and dismay that the author Toni Morrison had not won a National Book Award or the Pulitzer Prize. Among the authors who signed were Maya Angelou, Amiri Baraka, John Edgar Wideman, and John A. Williams (Terry McMillan was not one of the signers). The statement mentioned that Morrison "has yet to receive the national recognition that her five major works of fiction entirely deserve."

John Edgar Wideman said in an interview that the purpose of the letter was "number one, a tribute, and number two, an announcement that a group of black writers, thinkers, and intellectuals can speak collectively. There are times and occasions when that group needs to speak out on issues." He denied that the purpose of the letter was to influence the upcoming Pulitzer Prize for literature, which was to be presented in April 1988. Toni Morrison's *Beloved,* which had been published in 1987, had been a finalist for the National Book Award in 1987, but had been beaten out by *Paco's Story* by Larry Heinemann. *Beloved* did win the Pulitzer, though, in 1988.

(In another letter, published with the statement, the critic Houston A. Baker, Jr., and the poet June Jordan added that it was a shame that the late James Baldwin had also never received either award. "We grieve," they wrote, "because we cannot yet assure that such shame, such national neglect, will not occur again, and then, again.")

In November, just before Terry and the four others met to choose the winner, word got out that there were divisions and conflicts among the five panelists. A *New York Times* article published on November 27, 1990—the day the winners were selected—reported that the jurors were split by "deep ideological divisions" and that the deliberations reflected the recent changes in the publishing industry. "I came out of the selection process for finalists feeling that only a couple of the five books represent my tastes, preferences, and standards," Paul West complained, adding that the dividedness was between himself and William Gass on one side, and Philip Lopate, Terry, and Catharine Stimpson on the other.

The winner they picked was Charles Johnson, a black man, for *Middle Passage*. Set in early nineteenth-century New Orleans, *Middle Passage* is the story of Rutherford Calhoun, a freed slave, womanizer, and self-described thief and liar forced to flee the city because of bad debts and an unlucky romance. He stows away aboard a ship, only to find that it is a slave ship bound for Africa. Johnson spent six years researching the book, during which he studied virtually every seafaring novel written, as well as nautical dictionaries and slave narratives of the horrible ocean crossing.

Johnson became the fourth black writer to win the prize in its forty-year history: Ralph Ellison, whose *Invisible Man* won the prize in 1953, and two black women, both in 1983: Gloria Naylor for *The Women of Brewster Place* and Alice Walker for *The Color Purple*. Ralph Ellison was in the audience as Johnson received his award in a ceremony at the Plaza Hotel.

"I've been waiting my entire life for this," said Johnson. A native of Illinois, Johnson had been a cartoonist who published his first cartoon in a store catalog at age seventeen. In 1970 he published the first of two collections of cartoons and later that same year hosted a PBS television series on drawing called *Charlie's Pad*. Later, he became a founding member of several groups who launched a new academic discipline called Black Studies. In 1974, he published his first novel, *Faith and the Good Thing*, and in 1982 *Oxherding Tale* was released. His short story collection, *The Sorcerer's Apprentice,* was nominated in 1986 for the PEN/Faulkner award.

As his prize was announced, Terry—and editors from his publisher, Atheneum—stood up and cheered.

In the meantime, *Disappearing Acts* was selling even better than *Mama*. Terry, now a pretty well seasoned and fearless interviewee, was doing interviews to promote the book. Her coarse street language and smart-ass attitude that her friends, family, and students were already familiar with was now being displayed to viewers, readers, and fans all over America. Many were offended, but just as many had to admit that the sista was unapologetically enthusiastic about her work. The rhythm she had created, using each success to lead to another, was working smoothly. You couldn't deny that Terry McMillan was indeed creating her own reality.

Continually, she defended her characters and her writing. Her method, she explained, was to write from the heart, and to portray black people in real middle-class situations. "Zora's family was supportive. She has a middle-class, stable family and a support group. Franklin came from a stable middle-class household too, just not a very loving one."

Film rights for *Disappearing Acts* were sold to TriStar Pictures, which began the search for a black screenwriter and actors.

Meanwhile, back in Brooklyn, Leonard's feeling about the book had grown into real anger. He got on the subway to Manhattan and sat down with attorney Peter S. Gordon of the law firm Bedell & Feinberg on lower Broadway, and asked Gordon if he had a case. Gordon felt that he had.

In Kings County Supreme Court, Gordon filed a defamation lawsuit against Terry, her publisher Viking Penguin, and Simon & Schuster, which published the book in paperback. Welch, the plaintiff, charged that the main male character in the novel, Franklin Swift, was recognizably himself, and that the realistic way his three-year relationship with Terry (as the character Zora) was depicted, plus the fact that Terry dedicated the novel to their son, caused him emotional distress—for which he ought to receive four million, seven hundred fifty thousand dollars. In a twenty-eight-page complaint (which Terry's legal-secretarial eagle eye would have criticized for not having page numbers on it!), Gordon outlined the instances in the book that he says defamed Welch, the plaintiff, and assigned a dollar figure to each instance, thereby coming up with the total.

When news of the lawsuit broke, fiction writers and publishers nationwide waited nervously to see what would happen, because this was a lawsuit that could affect any writer of fiction in the country. The case was frightening, said novelist Marita Golden, "because some of the greatest fiction is based on real people. I think it's just part of the general nastiness of the time, that people see someone doing well and they want part of it. It's part of the whole intolerance of the imagination." If Welch won the case, she added, "it would definitely [have] a chilling effect on fiction writers."

Viking Penguin lawyered up too. Their law firm was the Madison Avenue firm of Frankfurt, Garbus, Klein & Selz, P. C. On advice of counsel, neither Terry—who did not dispute the case—nor Leonard said a word to the press while the lawsuit was pending. For the next several months, hundreds of pages of motions, stipulations, and affidavits were filed back and forth.

In statements to the press, Peter Gordon, Welch's lawyer, said that he and his client objected to the way the book allegedly portrayed Welch in a character named Franklin Swift, as "hostile, angry, and lazy," a "racist," someone who "drinks on the job" and is "intolerant toward homosexuals," a "stool pigeon," a "rapist," a "drug user," and "a man who is crazy and sick."

Martin Garbus, the attorney for Viking Penguin, was a well-known attorney who had for thirty years handled freedom-of-speech cases; his most famous was the 1964 trial of comedian Lenny Bruce, the best-known obscenity trial in history. He countered by calling Welch's action "a private passion, a vendetta." Yes, Terry and Leonard had lived together in Brooklyn for three years and had a child, as did Zora and Franklin in *Disappearing Acts,* Garbus noted. Nevertheless, he pointed out, "It is not so much a lawsuit as a marital dispute. If the book had been totally obscure and if Terry McMillan were an obscure writer, you would have a different case."

As for the monetary damages Welch demanded in the suit, Garbus called them "preposterous. Someone would have to be nearly driven out of work [in order to collect damages], and so far we have no reason to believe that has happened" to Welch, Garbus said. While there were some similarities between Leonard Welch and Franklin Swift, such as the fact that both were tall black construction workers, Garbus said, "What Terry McMillan has done is no different than what other writers have done. It has to be permissible to draw on your real-life experiences. Otherwise, you can't write fiction."

Welch's lawyer accused Terry's depiction of being too realistic. "If you're going to call it fiction, make it fiction." he said, adding that because of *Disappearing Acts* Welch "has been shunned in different areas. People have been looking at him differently, suspiciously."

Martin Garbus also knew a little about creating one's own reality: He had himself done that very thing. Martin's mother had died in a fire when Martin was three years old; Martin's father had lost eleven members of his own family, including his mother, father, brothers and sisters—in Polish concentration camps. Growing up in the Bronx, Martin and his father had only each other.

Although Martin's father had escaped Polish anti-Semitism, he could not forget the fear of persecution, and he taught his son that the safest thing to do was to remain "invisible and silent." So as little Martin worked in his father's tiny, claustrophobic candy store, he feared becoming like his father—and tried to dream of a way out. His escape came through joining the military, where, by way of his own court-martial for a petty offense, he first tested his belief in not being "invisible and silent." He never looked back.

In the meantime, Terry was in Arizona, teaching her writing class, giving interviews about the recently published *Breaking Ice* . . . and still bitching and moaning about how there were no good men around. Only, she continued to bitch and moan on paper. Viking wanted another novel, so Terry did what she did best: she wrote about what she knew. And at the moment what she knew was Where, Oh Where Are the Decent Men? So she wrote a story—set in Arizona, of course—about four black women: Savannah Jackson, a successful but love-starved television producer; Robin Stokes, an insurance company executive who cannot bring herself to break up with her liar and womanizer of a boyfriend, Russell; Bernadine Harris, Savannah's college roommate, whose successful, professional husband of eleven years announces that he is leaving her and the kids for his young, white bookkeeper; and Gloria Matthews, a full-figured hair salon owner whose weight problem may be connected to her fear of intimacy with a man. All these women are geniuses in the business world, but dunces in the man-woman relationship world.

The title of Terry's story was *Waiting to Exhale.*

Viking Penguin had given her a deadline of September 1, 1991, and had scheduled the book for May 1992 publication. But with the lawsuit, and the teaching, and the deadline, Terry was overworked. She decided that she would take a leave of absence from the University of Arizona in June, after the end of the spring 1991 semester.

On April 3, 1991, Judge Jules L. Spodek dismissed the case of *Welch v. Penguin Books USA Inc., Terry McMillan and Simon & Schuster Inc.* The entire publishing community breathed a huge sigh of relief.

In dismissing the suit, Judge Spodek found that while there were striking similarities between the character Franklin Swift and the ex-boyfriend Leonard Welch, Terry, in basing her character on Welch, did not libel or defame him.

The case turned on the fact that the character, Franklin Swift, was as abusive drunk who was sometimes lazy, hostile, racist, homophobic, and emotionally unbalanced, while "Leonard Welch is none of these things," Judge Spodek wrote in his ruling. People who knew Welch, the judge said, "had no difficulty differentiating him from Franklin Swift; the defamatory material was clearly not believed." Spodek added that it was accepted fact that novelists create fiction from their own lives and a reader would have to be totally convinced that a character in a book "is not fiction at all."

Lawyers for Viking Penguin said they believed the ruling would establish an important precedent and extend the freedom of artists.

"It's the broadest extension of any libel-action case in the U.S.," said Martin Garbus. "It's a tremendous victory in a case that could have gone the other way." Russell Smith, another Viking attorney, said Spodek's ruling would carry special weight because other courts around the country look to New York for precedents in publishing cases. "I would hope lawyers who would sue publishers to make a quick buck would realize it's a waste of time," he said.

Welch's lawyer, Peter Gordon, said only that he did not know if he would appeal the ruling.

Terry broke her silence on the matter and said in a telephone interview, "Undoubtedly I am quite relieved, not just for myself, but for other writers. I created a fictional character for which he was partially the inspiration. But, it is fiction. You make it up. This was a love story, written with love, and he knows it."

Martin Garbus knew a thing or two about recycling his experiences onto paper too: he turned his victory in the case into an article for the *New York Law Journal,* in which he noted:

The world's most renowned authors and playwrights, including William Faulkner, James Joyce, Leo Tolstoy, Eugene O'Neill, Fyodor Dostoyevsky, and Ernest Hemingway have all drawn upon their knowledge of actual persons to create fictional characters. Literary critics have observed that this is the case with all great fiction, and that artificially constructed characters divorced from an author's real life inevitably ring hollow.

Garbus went on to describe how writers like Faulkner, O'Neill, Hemingway, and Jack Kerouac all drew on their experience with real people (family, friends, lovers) and by reconstructing, dissecting, and making thinly disguised portraits of them, created some of the best novels and plays ever written. Terry was in good company.

By the end of the summer of 1991, the lawsuit behind her, Terry had moved back to California. Madeline chose to remain in Tucson, where her asthma didn't bother her so much.

Even as she moved, Terry was in the middle of writing *Waiting to Exhale*.

"I had the movers take my computer last," she said in an interview. "They were putting books in boxes, and I was sitting there writing. I get to California, I'm sitting in my sister's fiancé's office going blind writing on my little laptop that's not backlit, I'm looking for a place to live while my furniture's on a truck somewhere, it's the end of August, and I'm supposed to be finishing the book by September 1!"

She later described the writing process: "I'm not one of these writers who just edits, especially when I'm working on a first draft. Sometimes I actually delete an entire chapter from the memory so I have to type it all over, because that's the only way I can relive it. I have to stay close to these people, I have to have their experiences too, and the only way to do that is to start all over—that stuff is cumulative. It can be very exciting, and it can be very painful, but I have to make the emotional investment. After about ninety pages of *Exhale*, I'm saying to myself, 'Are they going to think this is as good as *Disappearing Acts?* Are they going to be disappointed?' Eventually, I just had to say, 'I cannot think about my audience; I can't guess what people are going to like.' "

With all the goings-on, it was clear that Terry was going to miss her September 1 deadline for submitting *Waiting to Exhale,* and she was not one to miss a deadline. During the process, she shipped off copies of the work in progress to her friend Doris Jean Austin for some professional criticism, her sister Crystal, and a few other friends. She also sent it to two of her girlfriends to read. "I wanted to make sure they didn't think any of the characters sounded like them." The first draft was finished by November 20, two months late; she sent Viking the final draft in December. This time Terry's dedication read, "This one's for you, Daddy: Edward Lewis McMillan, 1929–1968."

In the meantime, Terry's style and look had changed from plain to striking. Her curly hair was cut into a fade (short on the sides and high on top), she wore colorful designer clothing, and indulged herself in the hugest earrings she could find, one-of-a-kind pieces that she found in various boutiques during her travels. Making sure she treated herself well, she kept her home filled with fresh flowers and paintings and sculptures by black artists that she purchased from galleries around the country while on book tours. Among the artists whose work she owned were John

Rozelle, Betye Sarr, Mary Lovelace O'Neal, Alexander Skunder, Joe Sam, Lamerol Gatewood, and Synthia St. James.

"I buy only what I really like," she said of the art that she favored. "I want my paintings to reflect my life. I especially like abstract art because I can bring something to it. No one tells me what to feel."

A year before, she had bought a Synthia St. James painting, a depiction of a regal group of women entitled *Ensemble*. Living with it every day, she decided she would like to use it for the cover of *Waiting to Exhale*. She called the artist, whom she'd never met, to request her permission.

Synthia and Terry, both struggling creative artists, had much in common. Synthia had done everything from writing bios for recording artists at CBS/Epic Records, to modeling and acting, to accounting, to writing ad copy, to running her own tax consulting business. By the time Terry called asking to use the painting, Saint James was just beginning to move into more public circles: a book-club edition cover for a collection of Alice Walker's writings, Richard Pryor's purchase of five prints for his new Bel Air digs, a poster for the Mark Taper Forum 1990 production of *Miss Evers' Boys,* a show in Paris.

St. James was committed to making her work affordable. Thus, she also created T-shirts, baseball caps, embroidered turtlenecks, clocks, watches, wooden coffee table boxes, children's books, and playing cards that could showcase her colorful ideas.

In the beginning of 1992, movie studios were beginning to bid for the film rights to *Waiting to Exhale*.

"My first thought was, I don't care [about selling the rights]," Terry said. "My second thought was I didn't think it would make a really good movie. I just couldn't picture it." But after giving it more thought, she realized that as a love story, it would be a departure from the usual black movies that Hollywood was making, which were largely homeboy-from-the-'hood type movies. "We don't have many love stories on the big screen," she mused, and decided to grant the movie rights to Twentieth Century Fox. Her fee was reportedly "comfortably" into the six figures—not bad for a poor black girl from Port Huron. One of the selling points was that Fox agreed to give her co-executive-producer status. The producers were Deborah Schindler and Ezra Swerdlow.

Then, Fox asked her to write the screenplay for the book. Remembering her neverending experience with writing the screenplay for *Disappearing Acts,* she declined, suggesting that Fox get another writer, which they did. But when they submitted the finished screenplay to Terry for her approval, she couldn't provide it. "I don't want to dog the sister," Terry said in an interview, "so I'll just say I wasn't happy with what she did." The script sat there, for eighteen months.

In the meantime, the studio tried to get Terry to reconsider writing the screenplay. Reconsider she did, but this time she said that she wanted assistance, that she wanted to collaborate instead of doing it alone. The ideal collaborator, she decided, would be able to structure a film, and wouldn't have the same emotional attachment to the story that she did.

Terry turned to her friend, the writer Amy Tan, who had written the 1989 best-seller *The Joy Luck Club*. Born in Oakland, California, to parents who immigrated to the United States from China, Tan was educated at San Jose State University and the University of California at Berkeley. She worked as a consultant to programs for disabled children from 1976 to 1981 and as a reporter, editor, and freelance technical writer from 1981 to 1987.

The Joy Luck Club, Amy's first novel, examined, in a series of sixteen stories, the experiences of and tensions between four Chinese-born immigrant women and their American-born daughters. The book alternates the voices of the mothers with those of the daughters: The mothers' stories tell of Chinese women's struggles against traditional female roles and family domination; the daughters tell of young professional women in the United States who strive for equality in their personal relationships and careers.

The Joy Luck Club had been a hit movie in 1993. Terry had enjoyed the movie, and asked Amy to explain how she had done it. Amy replied that writing the script had been a positive experience, because she had collaborated with a screenwriter named Ron Bass on the movie. Bass had also written the screenplay to the Academy Award–winning *Rain Man.*

"I figured if he could be Chinese, he could be black," quipped McMillan. She got on the phone and called Ron Bass to invite him to help.

Ron Bass had become a bookworm when he was bedridden with high fevers and dizziness as a child. "I was in bed from age three to eleven, for the first four years all the time," Bass explained in an interview. Although his illness was never diagnosed, little Ron used the time well: He taught himself to read at age three, and began writing short stories at six. Apparently this intelligence was rewarded: He attended Harvard Law School and became an attorney—until Hollywood beckoned. He co-wrote the screenplay for the film *Rain Man,* which won him an Oscar in 1988. Among the other hits he wrote were *Sleeping with the Enemy, Dangerous Minds, When a Man Loves a Woman,* and *The Joy Luck Club*—all movies in which he spoke for women.

When Terry asked him to collaborate with her on *Waiting to Exhale,* he accepted her invitation. It was a relatively smooth collaboration, which Terry later described: "I'd sit down and do the writing. Then Ron would come in and help me figure out what scenes to leave and what works and what doesn't. He's a good technician. When you've written the novel, it's hard to distance yourself from the work. Ron helped me connect the dots. That's why it didn't matter that he wasn't black."

Bass outlined the book and the scenes, and set page limits per scene. McMillan wrote, faxed him the pages, and then the two talked it over by phone. "Fortunately, we're both morning persons," she said. "I couldn't have worked with a night person. And we had similar work habits. It was smooth all the way. He wants to work all the time."

"I hate to leave anything undone," Bass said.

"Me, I'm someone who never likes to quit in the middle," Terry said. "We had a good rhythm. We'd never end up the phone calls mad. We'd always patch up our disputes."

Although Bass kept Terry's voice intact, he needed to alter the story line for structural purposes. She had no problem with it, Bass said, "no ego about the story. She would have changed even more."

"Writers are usually hesitant to let go," Terry said. "But my attitude is that I've already had my characters and let them say what I wanted. I don't have some emotional attachment to these ladies; I didn't feel like I owned them or they were my possessions. They sort of feel like offspring. I was really able to separate the movie characters from those in the novel. I did not fight for certain scenes as many authors do. I went into the project knowing stuff would get lost."

Two drafts later, it was time to assemble a crew and cast. Terry was glad the writing part was over. Naturally, she wanted a black person to direct the film, and made her preference known. Julie Dash, who directed *Daughters of the Dust,* was Terry's recommendation. While the studio said no to that suggestion, they said yes to Forest Whitaker.

Whitaker was a stocky, six-foot-tall, mild-mannered actor and former college football player, best known for his performance as Jody, the captured soldier in the 1992 hit movie *The Crying Game.* A Los Angeles native whose father sold insurance and whose mother was a schoolteacher, Whitaker attended the University of Southern California as a voice major. He switched to theater, and won a scholarship to the Drama Studio in Berkeley, California. At twenty-two, he made his acting debut as a football player in the 1982 comedy *Fast Times at Ridgemont High,* which also starred Jennifer Jason Leigh, Sean Penn, and Phoebe Cates. Later, director Clint Eastwood cast him in the starring role of *Bird,* the 1988 Charlie Parker biographical movie. Whitaker also worked with Martin Scorsese in the 1986 film *The Color of Money,* Spike Lee in 1989's *Do the Right Thing,* Oliver Stone in the 1986 movie *Platoon,* and Barry Levinson in 1987's *Good Morning Vietnam.*

Considering the criticism she had received for the way men were treated in the book, Terry thought it would be "refreshing" to have a black man direct a movie about four black women. But of course she was criticized for that too, and she had to go into defensive mode. This time she was a little more edifying.

"I've been approached by people who want to know, Why did you get a man to direct *Waiting to Exhale?* But it's not about gender, it's about his understanding of the work." She picked Whitaker because "He's intuitive and sensitive, and he liked those women. He didn't come into the project with some other agenda. I didn't write the Bible; this is a story about four black women and it's supposed to be fun."

Whitaker's take on it was that "It's the women in the book who chose certain men who cause them to end up in painful circumstances. As the title suggests, you are talking about people who don't even know how to breathe or feel good about themselves. But luckily, it's the friendship among them that takes them each on a journey of transformation. I never felt like the difficulty of my directing this story is that I'm not a woman. I can only tell the story as I see it and perceive it."

It also helped that at the time, he was engaged to be married to one Keisha Nash. "Making a film about learning to feel good about yourself, your friendships, and your relationships was very appealing to me," he said.

As for the cast, Whitaker's first choice was for Whitney Houston to play the role of Savannah. This was the second acting gig for Houston after her debut in the 1992 movie *The Bodyguard,* in which she starred as a singer-actress who hires a former Secret Service agent, played by Kevin Costner, as her personal protector after she receives threatening letters from a disturbed fan. The film grossed $400 million worldwide. Angela Bassett, who had been nominated for an Academy Award for her role as entertainment-industry survivor Tina Turner in the 1993 film *What's Love Got to Do with It?,* was cast in the role of Bernadine Harris. Whitaker wanted to give the other two roles to lesser-known actresses, because, he said, "the opportunities for black actresses are much more limited than for other actors. I hope the success of this film will create more opportunities for black actresses. They are the most underused talents in the acting profession." Thus, the role of Robin Stokes was given to Lela Rochon, who previously appeared in the comedy movies *Harlem Nights* (1989) *Boomerang* (1992), and *Meteor Man* (1993); and the part of Gloria Johnson was given to Loretta Devine, one of the stars of the Broadway play *Dreamgirls.*

While the cast and crew were getting hired and reading the script, Whitaker was carefully plotting the other aspects of the film. How the scenes would be shot was planned with Whitaker and his director of photography, so that by the time they got on the set, Whitaker would know what the shots would look like.

....

On May 28, 1992, the hardcover edition of *Waiting to Exhale* was released, with its first printing of 85,000 copies hitting the bookstores. In the publishing industry, there was a $700,000 floor (that is, minimum purchase price) for the paperback rights, which were eventually purchased by Pocket Books, a division of Simon & Schuster. Terry got ready to go on a huge twenty-city, six-week tour—that Viking sent her on—beginning in the West with a breakfast speech at the annual American Booksellers Association convention (known in the industry as the ABA) in Anaheim, California, and ending with a July reading at Central Park's SummerStage festival. In between were almost thirty bookstore appearances on the itinerary, one of which was in Port Huron.

No one, anywhere, was prepared for the commercial success of *Waiting to Exhale*. By the end of 1992, over 700,000 hardcover copies of the book had been sold and the paperback rights had been purchased for $2.64 million—a record figure for a novel by an African American author and one of the highest sums ever paid to any writer at that time. Terry had also recorded a three-hour abridged audio version of the book.

The way Terry McMillan was treated now was a far cry from the way she had been treated as a first novelist, back in 1986. She had made a name for herself as an important contemporary novelist with a considerable following, so she was treated that way. There were publicists, editors, and accounting department people who knew her name and who took care of her. (But Terry kept up with all the numbers involved in her career: numbers of books sold, royalties earned, rights sold. Girlfriend did not play.) During her book tours, she stayed at the best hotels.

Masseuses were provided by the publisher to massage her tired autographing hand. She was picked up in cars and taken around by escorts hired by the publishing company to accompany authors from place to place.

One of Terry's escorts, a black woman, gave her some feedback and some advice. " 'Girl, I don't know what your next book is going to be about, but please, please, I beg you, don't start going to get all deep on us. Please don't start floating and decide now you're going to write the book of life. Please keep doing it just the way you've been doing it and tell us the stories that we can relate to because that's what we need, so don't start switching up on us.' I will never forget that, ever forget that," Terry said.

"I don't think I can keep this pace," she said. "I'm really not used to being so celebrated. I don't even believe the stuff that's happened so far. It's wonderful, it's a writer's dream, but it doesn't really feel like it's happening to me. 'There's this chick I know named Terry McMillan, and gee, I can't wait to read this *Waiting to Exhale*—it sounds like a good book!' "

Whenever she entered a bookstore or auditorium to do her readings, she commented that she felt like a preacher at a revival meeting. Hours before the appointed time, her fans—mostly black women who were students, professionals, homemakers—began lining up, clutching copies of the book. As she read from the book, the crowds rarely sat quietly listening. They made themselves some noise, often drowning her out.

"You tell it, girl!"

"Ain't that the truth!"

"You can say that again, sister!"

"Amen!"

"It doesn't get much better than that, hearing that kind of reaction to your book," she said. "It feels like being in church. You know, we have this call-and-response thing in the black church, people crying out when the preacher talks. 'Yes, I hear you! You're talking to me!' Black audiences let you know how they feel. They don't hold back. I love it."

During Terry's appearances on radio call-in shows, the same thing happened: The phone lines jammed in a telephonic version of the auditorium scenario, with fans calling to tell her how much her book was like "sitting in the living room with a glass of wine, talking to my girlfriends."

And yes, she got her wish: She was finally on the Oprah Winfrey show. "Don't you love it when you read a book and you're laughing out loud?" enthused Oprah about *Waiting to Exhale.* "It's like a conversation with your girlfriends, but you don't have to pay the long-distance phone bills."

Both ordinary readers and literary critics agreed that the dialogue was so true to life that they found themselves immediately drawn into the character's lives. In her review for the *New York Times Book Review,* novelist Susan Isaacs, who is white, agreed. Comparing the book to the 1963 novel *The Group* by Mary McCarthy and the 1958 novel *The Best of Everything* by Rona Jaffe ("the best of its predecessors . . . about female buddies"), Isaacs said that "McMillan's heroines are so well drawn that by the end of the novel, the readers is completely at home with the four of them . . . reading *Waiting to Exhale* is like being in the company of a great friend. It is thought-provoking, thoroughly entertaining, and very, very comforting."

In her review for the *Times Literary Supplement,* Frances Stead Sellers wrote, "Her characters' preoccupation with deodorants, douches, and dates soon grows wearisome . . . but whether her views are politically correct or not, McMillan has hit a nerve. Many African-American women identify with her heroines. Its one true importance is that it appeals to a market that American publishers have previously overlooked—the new black middle class. But its literary merits are modest."

And of course, there was that damned profanity. The *Publishers Weekly* starred review (the star "designates books of unusual interest and merit") warned, "Indeed, the novel's major drawback may be the number of times such words as *shit, fuck,* and *ass* are repeated on every page."

But Terry had her defenses up for that one. "So what? That's the way we talk. And I want to know why I've never read a review where they complain about the language that male writers use!

"Sometimes you get these real prissy types who pretend like they've never heard any of these words, and they say, 'I don't know why Miss McMillan felt she had to portray black women speaking such vulgarities.' But the truth is, if you eavesdrop on peoples' conversations, we abuse language. We don't always speak correctly, and we often use words that we wouldn't want our children to use. And girl, this book isn't about how we would like to see life. It's about how life really is."

Another criticism was of the novel's emphasis on brand

names—BMW, Coach leather goods, Federal Express, ESPN, Tic Tacs, Pop-Tarts, Jeep Cherokee, Rossignol skis, Mc-Nuggets, Calvin Klein, and Perrier are only a fraction of the names peppered throughout the book.

For regular Terry fans and probably also for readers for whom this was a first Terry experience, seeing brand names every few pages was a little jarring. It would be as if, for example, in her biography *Dust Tracks on a Road,* Zora Neale Hurston had written "He handled bales of cotton like Louis Vuitton luggage" instead of "He handled bales of cotton like suitcases." Or "The axe was still over her shoulder, but now it was draped with Uncle Jim's Armani pants, Calvin Klein shirt and Kasper coat" instead of "The axe was still over her shoulder, but now it was draped with Uncle Jim's pants, shirt and coat." Except throughout the whole book. Usage of brand names can date a book quickly. But of course the other side of that argument is that they can provide a look at history and cul-cha.

Often, advertisements in *Writers' Digest* and other writers' magazines are placed by manufacturers to implore writers that as the names of their products are trademarked and copyrighted, writers must use service marks or trademarks alongside any usage of the name. Well, *Waiting to Exhale* must have driven them crazy!

Like it or not, the brand names were there. Instead of splashing on perfume, the character Savannah "splashed on puddles of Joy" as did Robin, who "sprinkled Halston" on her pillowcases, or a stranger at a bar wore too much Polo. Savannah sucked on not a breath mint, but a Tic Tac. Bernadine's husband John's vehicles were not two luxury cars and an SUV, but a BMW,

Porsche, and Cherokee; in their home were not fixtures, appliances, pots, and pans, but Kohler toilets, a Sub-Zero refrigerator, Krups coffee maker, Cuisinart food processor, and Calphalon cookware. And in their wardrobes were not watches and luggage, but Rolex, Seiko, and Louis Vuitton. And on and on. This could break up the flow of the story, but that's the way Terry wrote it and that was her voice. It couldn't have been so bad, anyway. With the proceeds from the book girlfriend could now purchase every living brand name she wanted from that list and beyond!

Because the male characters in the book were deceitful, conceited, or dependent on drugs, Terry expected to be accused of "black-male-bashing." But on that issue there wasn't too much fallout.

The book stayed on best-seller lists for over a year, and rekindled interest in *Disappearing Acts* and *Mama*. *Disappearing Acts* was made into a three-hour, two-cassette audio book in 1993. The chapters narrated by the character Zora were read by Terry, and those narrated by the character Franklin were read by Avery Brooks, a sexy-voiced actor best known for his television roles in the series *Spenser: For Hire* and *Star Trek: Deep Space Nine*. His theater credits included title roles as Othello and Paul Robeson, so he was well qualified. *Mama* was rereleased as a mass market paperback in 1994. Both the *Disappearing Acts* tape box and the *Mama* paperback featured cover art by Synthia St. James.

Clara Villarosa, the African American owner of Hue-Man Experience Bookstore in Denver, said "The people who bought

Exhale, I felt, were women who really identified with the characters. They don't consider her like an Alice Walker or a Toni Morrison. She's writing more about *their* experience.

"When you look at the literature of Toni Morrison or Alice Walker, a lot of it reported on experiences in rural areas, or back when. Contemporary black fiction, in a black woman's voice, was a total void. These women weren't reading the Toni Morrisons. They'd say, 'Honey, I want it to sound like me.' And when it did, they loved it."

As one woman reader put it, "I love Toni Morrison and Alice Walker, but they can be difficult to understand. I read *The Bluest Eye* twice before it made sense, and then I still think I missed some of it. I never had that problem with Terry."

Another, agreeing, added "I admire those writers, but damn, they depress me. I know we've been victims as black women, but Alice and Toni really stick it to you and I don't want to be reminded of it all the time. Terry talks about problems, but with humor and fun. I laugh through the tears. That's what I need."

Indeed, Terry's readers wore the latest hairstyles and clothing and looked elegant and impeccable. They were consumers with disposable income, and they spent it on homes, cars, music, cosmetics, and designer clothes. This was a new untapped market that the publishing industry had ignored. These readers, suggested one article, "were delighted to find that hair weaves, press-on nails and admiration for Janet Jackson's buttocks have a place in fiction."

Reader reaction to *Waiting to Exhale* was plentiful. Most readers were struck by the fact that it was a book that every black woman could relate to, and told the truth about black men and women's relationships. It also, they said, provoked never-ending discussions about the issue. Some readers reported (bragged?) that they read the book while having sex.

Men who read it found themselves admitting that yes, some of their friends were like the men in the book. But they cautioned not to forget that the women had their eyes open, they just picked losers. Others commented on the universal theme: Many people would think the book was about black women, but it was more far-reaching than that.

There were some black critics who got on Terry's case for not writing about racial conflict. Thulani Davis, writing in *The Village Voice,* suggested that McMillan was deliberately turning her back on politics and true art: "Her work will continue to raise questions among African Americans about the fuzzy line between realism and popular misconception," wrote Davis, calling the novels of Terry McMillan and three other authors "more bup art than black art" ("bup" being a nickname for buppie, which is an acronym for black urban professional). Terry's response was that the Davis analysis was "insulting," and called black critics "our worst enemies. We have not forgotten the struggle that came before."

Other black critics scolded Terry for choosing a white Jewish male to co-write the screenplay. On the other side of the coin, the Jewish press put the reverse question, although not so menacingly, to Bass. The headline for a January 11, 1996, article in the *Metrowest Jewish News* read "Jewish Writer Speaks for Black Women in *Exhale.*" For the article, Bass was asked if it was unusual that a Jewish man could provide an insight into the Asian American and African American female psyches, as he did with Amy Tan and Terry's projects.

Bass pointed out that he had unmarried Jewish women friends, who never met the right guy, who could relate to the bad-relationship-prone Savannah. As for Bernadine, he said that "She has given up so much in her life to support her successful husband, who then leaves her for a younger woman. What she goes through is what a lot of women—Jewish women in-cluded—go through."

The black women of *Waiting to Exhale* had something that Bass himself could relate to in a way. "I know that feeling of insecurity," he said. "I know the fears. I'm a very inse-cure person."

Bass said that he suspected that the basic difference between men and woman was that women want to know what's inside men, even if it screws them up. Men, on the other hand, admire the finish line, not what got them there, he said. Even Jewish men, who "can be very sensitive, compassionate, probably more than the average man. Still, they're result-oriented."

In the publishing industry, *Waiting to Exhale* had another signif-icant role. In 1992, it was the first time in publishing history that books by three black women were all in the top ten on the *New York Times* fiction best-seller list: In addition to *Waiting to Ex-hale,* Alice Walker's novel *Possessing the Secret of Joy* and Toni Morrison's novel *Jazz* and book of essays *Playing in the Dark.*

"Publishers discovered that they had been leaving money on

the table" by not recognizing there was a market for books by black authors, black author Bebe Moore Campbell said, noting that the publishing industry was forced to give up three myths: blacks don't read; blacks don't buy books; and whites don't buy books written by or about blacks.

"These books have to appeal to whites, too, in order to land on the best-seller list," observed Clara Villarosa.

"Immediately, each publishing company wants to duplicate that success," said Ken Smikle, publisher of *Target Market News,* a Chicago-based trade publication which covers black consumer marketing, suggesting that Terry had started a new industry.

Another wake-up call for publishers that was made by *Waiting to Exhale* was that black readers and white readers are reached in different ways; the usual methods of publicity and promotion to white audiences need to be adjusted for black audiences. "So much depends on the connection to the community," said book publicist Vaneese Lloyd-Sgambati. "The biggest thing with us is word of mouth. At eight in the morning most African Americans aren't watching TV. They're on their way to work. So radio's a better way to getting the message across."

By 1993 Terry McMillan had officially become a celebrity: "I'm just starting to get used to hearing my name called when I'm in some strange place. But also, it's been a little overwhelming. I started getting scared. In each city, I was frightened at the size of the audience. I couldn't believe all of these people were coming to hear me read from this book and get theirs signed. It's the highest form of flattery. It sort of let me know I did something right."

She didn't take her financial security for granted, either. Not one to be exploited, she kept on top of every penny. "Solomon started saying, 'You know, Mom, people at my school say you're famous and we're rich.' Every once in a while I'll lie and say, 'We don't have any money.' Or if he asks for things I'll say 'We can't afford it.' I came from a school where you had to work for what you wanted. So he can do his chores and save his allowance. When he wants another Nintendo game, he can buy it. I suppose by normal standards, I could be considered rich, but I don't carry myself that way. I don't spend it that way. I don't take it for granted."

Of course, there was no shortage of strangers who wanted to share in some of Terry's wealth. Charities solicited her for contributions and relatives wanted her to make appearances at their children's schools, or they called and asked her for money, especially at graduation time ("Well, you know Felicia's doing good in school . . ."). "I regret all the attention," she said once in as interview. "I get so many calls, from black women who are trying to get themselves through college, from crackheads who want clothes for their babies. I get asked for things all the time. Every now and then, I send [ex-boyfriends who are not doing so well] checks just to perk them up."

Her sister Vicki's son—and her namesake—Colorado State wide receiver Terrence Zenno, was invited to the VIP party for the New York premiere of *Waiting to Exhale*. "My auntie is supportive of all her nieces and nephews," he told an interviewer. "The one thing she can't tolerate is poor grades. As long as you are doing something positive, she's going to reinforce it.

It might be a card to show she cares and is thinking of you. It works just as well with me. I work to the bone to let her know I'm trying."

Terrence enjoyed *Waiting to Exhale.* "I just think any man secure in his manhood can watch the movie and laugh. Every man is not like the ones the movie portrays. I'm not going to say there are no men in the world like that. A certain percentile fits that mold. If you fit that mold, you're not going to like the movie. I'm not just prejudiced because it's my aunt. If Danielle Steel had written it, I would have enjoyed it just as much."

"If I said 'yes' to everything I was asked to do, I could forget about writing another book," Terry said. "For a while, I did say okay and I'd sell tickets or show up at something, but I got burned out. I cannot save the world, which for a while I think I was trying to do. I can't represent every organization, even though I believe in what they're doing. I still have a life."

Although Maya Angelou wrote that "you're one good, good writing sister," Terry has said that she still has not gotten the respect she longs for from Alice Walker or Toni Morrison, two of her other literary idols.

Even though Terry's work falls into the contemporary category and she is up to the minute on the topics she writes about and the characters in her books, she is extremely well read and her interest in authors spans far and wide. She has a great amount of respect and reverence for the classic black authors (Maya Angelou, James Baldwin, Toni Morrison, Zora Neale Hurston, Alice Walker, Margaret Walker). She does not view other writers as her competitors—or one another's competitors, for that matter; and one of the things she says she is proud of doing, both with her students and with her audiences and fans, is urging them to get out pen and paper so she can give them a list of other black writers to read. Her own support of other black writers was even more reason for Terry to expect the living black female writers *she* admired—specifically Toni Morrison, Gloria Naylor, and Alice Walker—to support her work by providing a quote or a blurb for *Waiting to Exhale.*

Now while Terry has said that she can't stand it when interviewers ask her what she thinks of Toni Morrison and Gloria Naylor and Alice Walker, as if all these contemporary black women writers are competitors (she feels that the media is trying to pit them all against each other), she is sensitive to the way she feels she is treated by these writers. Although she did get blurbs for *Waiting to Exhale* from her friends Spike Lee, Amy Tan, and Charles Johnson, she was disappointed that she couldn't get a blurb or a quote from Toni Morrison, Gloria Naylor, or Alice Walker. In her view, these writers weren't showing their support for her.

Sources say that when Terry sent one of her galleys to Alice Walker to request a blurb, the galley was returned to her by Walker's assistant with a form note. Apparently this hurt Terry's feelings, because in her view, it was not common practice for such galleys to be returned.

But the most hurtful thing happened in the fall of 1991, in San Francisco. Terry had taken seven-year-old Solomon to a book party at Marcus Books, a black-owned bookstore, for Alice

Walker's children's book *Finding the Green Stone,* which had been published in October. There, they met up with Terry's friend, the gay black novelist Randall Kenan, whose critically acclaimed novel *A Visitation of Spirits* had been published in 1989. Because of his great admiration for Alice Walker, Kenan had sent his new collection of short stories, *Let the Dead Bury Their Dead,* to her for a blurb. When he learned she would be in San Francisco, he made a special trip to the book party so that he could meet her in person.

At the party, when introduced to Kenan, Walker is supposed to have said something like, "Oh, I have something of yours but don't know when I'll get to it," and by so doing hurt Kenan's feelings.

Later, in a question-and-answer session following the event, Terry raised her hand to ask Walker a question about her forthcoming novel (which was *Possessing the Secret of Joy,* as it happened, with the theme of female genital mutilation, which would be published in June of 1992). Walker answered, "That's true," and said nothing further—leaving Terry feeling dissed. Afterward, confused because she didn't she feel she deserved that, Terry went up and introduced herself to Walker, mentioning that she'd asked that question because she'd thought Walker's fans might want to know about it. "They'll find out soon enough" were Walker's only words to Terry.

But Alice Walker is herself sensitive. In a 1979 memo to the editors of the *Black Scholar,* in defense of the writers Ntozake Shange and Michele Wallace, Walker admitted that "One of my own great weaknesses . . . is a deep reluctance to criticize other black women. I am much more comfortable praising them. Surely there is no other group more praiseworthy, but on the other hand, no other group is more deserving of justice, and good criticism must be, I think, simple justice." And in her 1987 essay "All the Bearded Irises of Life: Confessions of a Homospiritual," Walker states how she was deeply hurt when her close friend, who was a lesbian, did not treat her as if she could be trusted to understand anything about her lesbianism. "Aquarians, they say [she wrote], can tolerate anything but being thought narrow-minded. In my case, this is certainly true."

Not to mention the relentless attacks Walker had gotten on her book *The Color Purple* and its subsequent movie for the way black men were portrayed in the work. "I felt thoroughly trashed for many years, because the attacks didn't just happen around the showing of the film; they continued for a long time. The only way I could keep going was to stay in my work. Black men—not all black men, but the ones who were violently opposed to my work—I think were dealing out of ego and were unable to even see the male characters that I had created."

Silly, then, to try to interpret another's reactions without knowing all the facts.

But Alice Walker did hear Terry's complaints and finally addressed the situation once and for all in her 1997 book of essays *Anything We Love Can Be Saved: A Writer's Activism,* in an essay called "This That I Offer You" (subtitled "People Get Tired; Sometimes They Have Other Things to Do"). The essay is, in essence, Walker's response to those who complain that she has ignored them—particularly to one black female writer. Although Walker gives this black female writer the pseudonym of Anna Caday, the writer is in fact Terry McMillan. Walker writes:

> Recently, I've been alternately irritated and puzzled by Anna Caday's various accounts of feeling "shunned" by me . . . Here is a woman whose books are selling spectacularly. She is witty, poised, attractive. People like her and appreciate her work. She has lots of money. A child. Friends. Her health. Her cup, in short, runneth over. And yet I find in *Essence,* as in *The New York Times* and even in the *Times* of London, that with all this, she still needs something from me and from Toni Morrison. What can it possibly be?

Walker goes on to mention that she had written a note of congratulations to "Caday" when Caday's novel—*Patience and Stress,* Walker pseudonames it in her essay—became a best-seller. Continuing, Walker refers to a *New York Times* article—she calls it "Caday's Carats," but it was in fact the article "McMillan's Millions," written by Daniel Max, which appeared in *The New York Times Magazine* of August 8, 1992. In the article, Max described Terry's feeling about the bookstore incident and noted that Walker declined requests to be interviewed for the article.

In her essay, Walker explains that she refused to talk to this "rude reporter" because she had not yet read the book, and that he was obnoxious, calling many times and upsetting her assistant. Then Walker provides her side of the bookstore incident, explaining that she felt it was inappropriate to talk about genital mutilation in front of an audience of children three to twelve years old.

And then Walker, admitting that she could now understand how "Ms. Caday" might have felt rejected or ignored, offers a story from her own life. She describes how, when she was in her early twenties, she met the great writer Langston Hughes, whom she idolized. They began a written correspondence, which they both enjoyed. But there came a time when she really needed to hear from him, and he did not answer an urgent letter she'd sent. Many thoughts went through her mind: Maybe he really did not like her. Maybe she'd made him angry. Maybe her letters bored him. Maybe he didn't like her writing. Or, being a black man, maybe he did not approve of her Jewish fiancé. Alice Walker kept thinking of things *she* might have done to *him*.

Finally, a couple of weeks later, she received a letter with his return address—but not in his handwriting. Inside was an invitation to his funeral.

He had died before receiving her letter.

We must learn to accept, as I had to then, that people get tired, cross, overworked, and overextended. They get PMS. Or, in Langston's case, prostate cancer. They get sick and sometimes they die. And none of it has anything, really, to do with us, and what we need or expect from them.

In other words, Terry, *relax* already.

....

Waiting to Exhale had started something with the reading public. Readers were hungry. They would read *Waiting to Exhale,* and then they wanted more. Bookstore owner Clara Villarosa watched it all happen, as readers began begging for similar books. "I'd say, read Bebe Moore Campbell," she said. "They'd come back wanting more. I'd say, read Tina McElroy Ansa, read Connie Briscoe."

And there *was* more—because by that time, Terry McMillan had opened the door for a new literary genre. Publishers, at long last seeing this huge market, had begun to publish black authors whose novels focused on relationships and problems of contemporary black people, especially women.

The predominant theme in their fiction was contemporary life, what's happening now. The old TV slogan "there are six million stories in the naked city" seems quite appropriate for today's black fiction authors who have simply taken their lives and put them on paper across all genres. And these stories are important because black readers can see this as a picture of their own lives. They can each see their day, at home (cleaning, taking care of babies, having a lover over, being sick, dying, getting high), at work (dealing with office politics, office affairs, career frustrations), at play (socializing, wanting to socialize), in love (in bed, making love, having foreplay, flirting, being mistreated and abused, fighting, killing) . . . the whole spectrum is now between book covers to be read about.

Who can say? If Terry had not been so blunt and raw in her

novels, would this black writing renaissance have happened? Wake up, of course it would. But Terry did open the door to if-she-can-do-it-so-can-I (writers) and if-this-book-by-this-black-author-can-sell-well-maybe-some-other-book-by-some-other-author can (white publishing community).

Terry was able to be a fly on the wall and give every little detail of our lives. Who could resist?

Even the bright-colored covers of the novels following hers were similar to Terry's *Waiting to Exhale*. Tina McElroy Ansa's *Ugly Ways* (1993) sold 92,000 hardcover copies. Connie Briscoe's *Sisters and Lovers* (1994) sold more than 100,000 copies in hardcover and 325,000 in paperback. E. Lynn Harris's best seller *And This Too, Shall Pass,* sold over 152,500 copies. There were more, and more to come—writers who did not focus on issues such as slavery, racism, or ghetto themes. The characters in their novels are interested in the American Dream of career, home, family, and romance.

No doubt about it: Terry McMillan cleared the path for other black female fiction writers. Now they could be offered five-figure book contracts and become famous—which they did, because hungry readers ate it up, with African Americans spending almost $300 million on books in 1995, according to Ken Smikle of *Target Market News.*

Benilde Little writes about upper-class blacks because she was "tired of ghetto blacks being held up as the authentic black person. I just refuse to buy that." Little, who grew up in Newark, New Jersey, graduated from Howard University. After a summer internship at the *Cleveland Plain Dealer,* she was a reporter for the *Newark Star-Ledger,* then spent five years at *People* magazine, after which she became an editor at *Essence* magazine.

Her first book, *Good Hair,* was a novel dealing with the lives of upper-class blacks. When she tried to find a publisher for it, the responses were, "We like the story, but we don't know that these people exist. Who's the audience?"

Little's attitude was, "The people in the book, the people in my life are not in any way related to the people you see in stupid black movies, except by pigment. The most destructive thing to happen to black Americans in the twentieth century [is] this idea that there is one black experience which revolves around not doing well in school, not speaking proper English, and somehow being connected to crime." Her book was finally published by Simon & Schuster.

Bebe Moore Campbell said that "Publishers realized that a lot of money could be made and it got their attention. Some publishers thought, Let's get another Terry, but more enlightened publishers realized the reading public didn't want copycat writers."

Connie Briscoe, when asked to whom she would compare herself, stated "Why must we always be compared? I think it's something they do because they just don't understand black writing, or they haven't read enough of it to be able to evaluate it on its own merit. So they compare it to something that they know, mostly Alice Walker, Toni Morrison, and Terry McMillan."

And when the readers finished the books, they still hadn't had enough. So they talked about what they had read. All over the country, black women began to form reading groups, or "sister circles," to discuss books like Terry's and the others that were flooding the market. Joining these groups were women of all types: professionals, entrepreneurs, educators, health care professionals, secretaries, attorneys, hairdressers, actresses . . . and on and on. The typical group meets once a month, each time at a different member's home, with the host providing refreshments or a meal. Every month, one member would get to choose the next book to be read. Some groups discussed literature by such authors as James Baldwin and other classic black writers.

The sister circles served a purpose higher than book discussion; they functioned as a social network, too, with members discussing politics, careers, and relationships, and generally nurturing each other, ultimately forming strong friendships.

But of course, not everyone was happy. In his publication *Quarterly Black Review (QBR)*, publisher Max Rodriguez, although pleased with the new crop of black authors and novels, lamented, "Where is the literature? Where are the seminal pieces that mark the passage of time in the life of a people? Where are the Langston Hugheses, the Ellisons, the Wrights, the Hurstons, and the Hansberrys?"

Well, the obvious answer to that query is that they are dead. Besides, those authors cannot be pluralized: there was only one Langston Hughes, one Ralph Ellison, one Richard Wright, one Zora Neale Hurston, and one Lorraine Hansberry.

Just as each author's work is unique and has a place in literature, so is each reader's interpretation and reception of a work.

Rodriguez's question suggested that he was a person who was sorely missing literary classics like those he mentioned. And that his definition of literature bears far more intellectual criteria.

Yet, there are other people out there. Nonintellectuals. The everyday person. There are people who only read nonfiction. There are people who begin reading in grade school, only read the classics, and have read them all by their thirties. Others don't read the classics until they are in middle age. There are people who have said (to the absolute shock of the intellectual), "I don't read many books." Terry didn't believe it either, until she met these people at her readings, and heard them say things like:

"Child, your book is the first book I ever finished in my life."

"I let my mama read it and then I let my husband read it—my husband don't read nothin', girl, and he read the whole book."

So it is very difficult and almost dangerous to set standards, because no two people are alike. The only standards that can be set are within a group of kindred spirits who all have the same criteria.

Indeed, each piece that a writer writes "marks the passage of time in the life of a people." Any book or article we read is reflective of the time in which it was written, even if inadvertently or peripherally; even Terry McMillan's use of brand names can be seen as a kind of time capsule

Perhaps the other side of Rodriguez's lament could be an exultation: Thank goodness there are more black writers out there, so many that the black writer has now become a force to be reckoned with by the white publishing community, as opposed to a rare figure who every year or so gets a book noticed by the mainstream publishing world. There are now authors who while maybe not clones of Langston Hughes, Ralph Ellison, Richard Wright, Zora Neale Hurston, and Lorraine Hansberry, are expressing their own voices: authors like E. Lynn Harris, Tina McElroy Ansa, Bebe Moore Campbell, Randall Kenan, Veronica Chambers, and many many others. There is room for all, and like it or not, Terry opened the door.

8

·····································

Getting the Groove Back

I was paid a lot of money. And that is where Waiting to
Exhale *has gotten too much credit. People started thinking,
Hey, you can get rich by writing a book. It wasn't a story that
motivated them. It was the money—and that is a sad-assed
reason to write a novel . . . I've gotten a lot of money because
God was on my side. I didn't know any famous writers
when I started writing. I wanted to tell stories. I could
have taught and paid the rent.*

—Terry McMillan

In the middle of her twenty-city *Waiting to Exhale* book tour,
Terry got lost in the San Francisco Bay Area of California—
and discovered a new neighborhood.

It was the Danville Area, a suburb about thirty miles east of
the Bay Area which includes the four communities of Alamo,
Blackhawk, Diablo, and the town of Danville. The area had one
of the lowest crime rates in the Bay Area, with zero homicides
in 1991 and 1992. Weather-wise, it was warmer than Oakland
and Berkeley, but cooler than other inland Bay Area cities. By

now well accustomed to nice neighborhoods, Terry was impressed with the cleanliness of the town. She learned that geographically, much of it was wooded, with many hiking trails and two large parks. Downtown, there were historic buildings, restaurants, delis, sidewalk cafes, and on some Sundays, the main downtown street closed for art fairs. Other amenities included community pools and a town theater. And during the holiday season, residents carrying lighted candles gathered downtown to walk to a large oak tree, trimmed with white lights, whose branches spread over Diablo Road. As they surround the tree, a switch is thrown, and the tree and then the downtown blaze into a cheerful holiday scene.

Checking further, Terry learned that Danville's academic rankings were among the tops in the state, generally in the ninetieth percentile. For kids, there were sports, the most popular of which were soccer and Little League, plus acting classes, dance classes, and exercise classes.

Real estate agents hyped the country atmosphere and crowed about the custom homes located in the best area of the town, which was in the western hills. Many of the homes boasted views of nearby Mount Diablo. There was even a literary ghost for Terry: The playwright Eugene O'Neill had written some of his best plays while living in those West Danville hills, and his home was preserved as a national monument. But neighbors of the O'Neill house sued to limit public visits to the home, to protect their privacy. Privacy . . . Terry liked that feature.

For Terry to end up living in Danville "was pure luck," she said. "I wasn't really planning to buy a house. I was just kind of looking. I'd talked to a realtor but planned nothing serious for a few months."

But the realtor showed her a house, and on impulse, liking its vibe, she purchased it in late 1992. It was a 4,800-square foot, five-bedroom, gray stucco custom-built home in the California/Mediterranean contemporary style. At the end of a quiet, dead-end street, it was surrounded by oak trees and rolling hills. From the front porch Terry could see deer on the hills and people riding horses along the trails. In the living room, there was a fireplace—by now an amenity that Terry had gotten used to. The house was very private, but the neighbors were very friendly.

"I walked in here, looked at the sunny rooms, and said, 'This is kind of nice,' " she told an interviewer. "I immediately started hanging my paintings, placing the sculptures and ceramics I collect. I wanted to make it my house, give it personality." Two such touches were a turquoise study and a raspberry bathroom.

Three months after she moved in, she began making changes to the house. The family room was renovated. The main stairway was rebuilt to fit the scale of the house. Doors, leading to a sheltered terrace, were built. She had the hill beyond the patio landscaped into an abundant garden, full of color.

In this house, Terry—who had been on the move practically all of her life, from the Port Huron days until now—finally felt she was in the first home in which she had ever felt rooted. The wanderlust was calming down: Life was fine. Terry had enough money to treat herself to the things that made life pleasurable, to the rewards of hard work: the home, a black BMW, a silver

Mercedes, and a navy Toyota Land Cruiser. Even her sister Rosalyn, who had been threatening to write a book, was beginning to do so.

And then tragedy struck.

In early September 1993, Terry treated her mother to a few things that would make *her* life pleasurable: a car, a house in Tucson, and "a mouthful of new teeth." Just a couple of weeks later, on September 30, Terry was on tour in Rome, Italy, promoting *Waiting to Exhale*. From her hotel room that evening, Terry spoke with Madeline, who was at Terry's house taking care of Solomon, now twelve years old. After the conversation, Terry went to bed.

Six hours later, she was informed that Madeline had died during an asthma attack. She was fifty-nine years old.

"I don't think I talked for ten hours after I heard," Terry later said. A thick blanket of sorrow drew over her, and she couldn't get out from under it.

Madeline Katherine Tillman's body was flown back to Port Huron for a funeral, which was held on Friday, October 8, at 1:00 P.M. at Mount Olive Baptist Church, two blocks from the Cleveland School where Terry had gone through her early school years. Reverend Anthony LaMarr Ross, the pastor of the Mount Calvary Missionary Baptist Church in Tucson, came to officiate. Terry shared Words of Expression, and her uncle LaVern Washington, associate pastor of the church, gave the eulogy. Madeline's nephews LaFonce McMillan, LaVern Washington, Jr., Arthur Dinkins, Demarr Dinkins, Tony Walton, and Kevin Walton, were pallbearers. Madeline was survived by her five children, eleven grandchildren, a great grandson, three brothers, and two sisters.

Adding to Terry's bereavement was a feeling of guilt because she had not always empathized with her mother about her asthma. For months, Terry was unable to function. "Do you know how hard it is to take your mother out of your address book?" She couldn't write, she couldn't make appearances. Family and friends, like her best friend Doris Jean Austin, helped her through it with calls and visits, even though Doris Jean herself hadn't been feeling so well and Terry had been urging her to go to the doctor. After about ten months had passed, Terry was beginning to emerge from the numbness.

Soon afterward, Doris Jean did go to the doctor. She was told that she had terminal liver cancer, and that it was beyond chemotherapy. Now that Doris Jean wanted to live, had a career and things to live for, she was being told what she had been ready to hear all those years ago following her first cancer diagnosis.

When Terry heard about Doris's diagnosis, she couldn't believe it.

On the Wednesday before Labor Day, 1994, wanting to make Doris as happy as possible while she was still around, Terry called her: "Doris, we going on a shopping spree, honey. Henri Bendel's. Tiffany's. Any fucking place you wanna go. You wanna go to London? You wanna go to Paris? You wanna go to Africa? Anywhere you wanna go. I'm not kidding. Doris, don't die on me, bitch, okay?"

The following weekend, the weekend after Labor Day, Doris

died. "I couldn't talk or move," Terry says. At Doris's funeral, which took place at the Walter B. Cooke funeral home on New York's Upper West Side, Terry sat in the front row and wept uncontrollably for her friend—and herself.

For the next few months, all she could do was to hope her mother and Doris would come back, or pick up the phone and call her to say it was all a big trick.

Seven months later, on April 10, 1995, Diane Cleaver, Terry's first agent, would die in her Manhattan apartment at the age of fifty-three.

But during all this, business went on. Terry was a big cheese now, and there was always some deal or other to be considered. Book-Of-The-Month Club had bought the rights to her next book—which was supposed to be *A Day Late and a Dollar Short*—sight unseen. And work on the movie *Waiting to Exhale*—the second major motion picture in recent years adapted from a black woman's novel (the first being Alice Walker's *The Color Purple* in 1985)—was beginning. Terry could not even rest.

In November 1994, two months after Doris Jean Austin's death, the filmmakers began scouting Phoenix locations for *Waiting to Exhale,* and Terry toured the city in a van with Ron Bass, Forest Whitaker, location manager Rick Rothen, and a representative from the Phoenix film office.

Rick Rothen and art director Marc Fisichella both lived in Arizona, and because the book was set in Phoenix, they wanted to give that city first choice for the location. The studio gave its approval to film the movie in Phoenix.

Actual filming of the movie began on February 28, 1995, and most of it was shot in Arizona. Phoenix bars, restaurants, hotels, homes, and apartment complexes were used, as well as locations in other cities, such as Scottsdale. The New Year's Eve finale scene was shot at Butcher Jones Beach, ninety minutes from downtown Phoenix. Terry only visited the set about six or seven times, as they were shooting during the school year and Solomon was in school. Besides, she put her trust in Whitaker and the rest of the crew, as she respected their abilities. She found it pretty boring to be on the set anyway.

"When you see how many times they shoot one scene, over and over and over again," she said, "you just know one of them is right. I would say to Forest, 'Didn't you like that one? Didn't you think that was perfect?' Next thing you know, they have to do the scene again. I was like, 'Hey, I have a video camera. I can get it for you, honey!' It was just so tedious!"

Music for the film was composed and written by Kenneth "Babyface" Edmonds, and artists who performed tunes for the soundtrack include R & B artists Toni Braxton, Aretha Franklin, Patti Labelle, Chaka Khan, and Mary J. Blige.

Style was important to the film, too.

As far as the characters' wardrobes was concerned, Whitaker and costume designer Judy Ruskin (whose credits included *Born on the Fourth of July, Sleepless in Seattle, A Walk in the Clouds,* and *Forget Paris)* decided to take a unique approach. After agreeing that the characters—working women, after all—would exhibit their own personal style instead of a designer's, "We decided that each woman was to represent an element and an aspect of nature," Ruskin said. Savannah would represent the wind; Robin would embody fire; Gloria would be earth; and Bernadine would be water.

Savannah, as wind, was dressed in loose pants, tunic sweaters, and unconstructed suits—clothes that had flow and movement; as an extra tongue-in-cheek touch, one of her outfits included pants with a cloud print. Robin, as fire, of course got to wear the reds and oranges—and sexy ones at that, such as a tight orange halter dress and a red lace bra. Gloria's earth wardrobe consisted of colorful blouses and tunics, and lots of accessories such as big hats. Bernadine got to dress in clear neutrals, mostly ivory, and no accessories: clean and clear, like water.

Although there were a few designer pieces in the wardrobes, most of the clothing was purchased at discount clothing stores. "Any sensible woman [like these characters] would go to Loehmann's or Marshall's or Ross Dress for Less" first, Ruskin said. "I got almost everything at Loehmann's. I'm the queen of bargains."

Art lover that she was, Terry's eye helped with some input for the sets, just as it had for the cover of the book.

During her gallery visits, she had befriended Sandra Berry, who owns the Neighborhood Gallery. On display there were some paintings by a young artist named Paul Deo, a former New York graffiti artist. Deo had gotten his big break when film director Spike Lee spotted his wearable art designs. "I was selling on the street outside a building where he was editing a film," Deo told an interviewer. "He bought a few sweatshirts and then commissioned me to do more to sell in his store. And it was like, Boom! That started everything."

Deo's art—strong, bright colors, positive themes—had been featured in the movies *Malcolm X* and *Boomerang* and on the television programs *The Cosby Show* and *In Living Color*. His work had been exhibited at galleries as well as at the Whitney Museum in New York City.

Impressed, Terry wanted some of his work in the film, and notified the film's production designer. Berry was contacted, and four of Deo's paintings were used in the film. The one most loved, *Baby Sis,* was on Robin's bedroom wall in the movie. The painting depicts a little girl with a halo and an indecipherable expression standing on a chair, flanked by doves, a baby carriage, and the American flag. "You see what you want to in it," Deo said.

Whitney Houston ended up purchasing that painting. "It had actually been sold to a doctor in St. Louis," Deo said, "but Whitney really wanted it. The doctor said, 'I need this painting to be part of my life!' but who can deny a determined diva? Negotiations ensued and I guess the price was right because Whitney was the one who walked away with it."

In May 1995, *Waiting to Exhale* finished shooting. During the filming, Terry and producer Deborah Schindler had become friends. The next month, Terry took the first vacation of her life: She went to Jamaica to seek psychic renewal. "Doris's death and my mom's made me do a lot of things this past year. It was, Why not? You know, I could be dead.

"Even being this quote-unquote best-selling author and having a few extra bucks in the bank, it doesn't change anything. You're still car pooling, washing clothes—at least I do—and I'm still the caretaker and the nurturer. And then I just decided maybe I should do something for myself."

Jamaica is a place where a lot of black Americans go for their vacations. It's close to the United States, it's got beautiful beaches and turquoise water, the weather is hot and sunny all year, it's got sensuous music, it's got swaying palm trees, it's got breathtaking mountains and waterfalls, and it's got swanky resorts. But Jamaica is also an economically depressed, developing country, with portions of its population suffering extreme poverty on the other side of those swanky resorts; at times the economic and political depression have erupted into violence which makes worldwide headlines. For this reason, the resorts are all self-contained and gated, and visitors are cautioned not to go outside the property lest they see how the "other half" lives.

Many women return from Jamaica with stories of how hard it is for them to relax because the Jamaican men won't leave them alone. But Terry, who had never been to Jamaica before, went anyway. Stories like those were no big deal to her, if she heard them at all; after all, to each his own. No doubt there were women who went to Jamaica to experience the very situation that others complained of.

Most of Jamaica's hundreds of thousands of tourist visitors take their business to either Negril, Montego Bay, or Ocho Rios, the three big resort locations on the island. For this, her first vacation ever, Terry treated herself to the best resort on the island. It was the Grand Lido in Negril, a luxury resort fifty-five miles west of Montego Bay. Of the three towns, Negril has the youngest and coolest vibe, and a long reputation for "anything goes," with the twenty-three-acre Hedonism resort devoted to exactly that.

Terry chose the Grand Lido resort because it promised "the ultimate luxury vacation with superb accommodations and personalized service." Included in the price were the luxury accommodations—on twenty-two acres of elegantly manicured grounds and a two-mile crescent of white sand beach—all meals; premium brand cocktails, plus wine with lunch and dinner; land and water sports, including instruction and equipment rental; recreational activities; and entertainment. No tipping was allowed.

It was no small hotel. There were two-hundred suites, all with beachfront and garden views. Every suite was equipped with air conditioning, satellite TV, CD player, coffee maker, hair dryer, and complimentary laundry and dry cleaning service. The junior suites had a large bedroom with king-size bed or two twin beds, sunken living room and small balcony or patio. The one-bedroom suites had a large bedroom and separate living room. Then there were the one-bedroom beachfront luxury suites, eight of them with open courtyard and private Jacuzzi, walk-in closet and powder room.

The resort was built by John Issa—the pioneer of all-inclusive resorts in Jamaica—who had been a senator of Jamaica from 1983 to 1989. One of the key economic benefits he brought to the islands was the employment of Jamaicans at his resorts. Rather than importing hotel-trained staff from off the island,

Issa preferred to hire his employees from the communities surrounding the resorts and to train them from scratch. Of the more
than two thousand employees at Issa's six Jamaican resorts, the
number of non-Jamaicans could be counted on one hand.

But chilling out was Terry's goal. Arriving two months after
the end of the peak tourist season (although the official hurricane
season had just begun on June 1), she found it calming, and it
hit the spot. She jogged along the beach, exercised, and began
to relax. "The sun. The breeze. The weather. The sand. I enjoyed it all. I felt my mother's spirit close by," she said. "She
was telling me, 'I know you miss me, but you've got a life to
live. Have fun. It's okay.' She encouraged me to be receptive."

And then a man came on the scene. The path of Jonathan
Plummer, a bronze, six foot four, twenty-four-year-old Jamaican with big eyes, no accent, dark wavy hair, and a slight goatee,
crossed that of Terry's. One weekend, Plummer, who worked
at the nearby Sandals resort, came to the Grand Lido to hang
out with a friend of his who worked there. The two buddies
played volleyball and hung out, and talked like they always did.

Sources say that Plummer was from a relatively well-to do
family on the island. That his father, also named Jonathan Plummer, had been the manager of the New Yarmouth sugar estate
in the rural Jamaican town of Mandeville. As manager of the
estate (the function of which was to process sugar cane into
sugar), the senior Plummer was in charge of about seven hundred workers. Later, he left New Yarmouth to run his own farm
and served as president of the Jamaica Association of Sugar Tech-
nologists in the early 1990s and again in 1997–98.

So as such, Jonathan Plummer the younger was not exactly from a poor family. In fact, his family wanted and expected him to either become involved with the family sugar interest or go to medical school. But Jonathan wasn't interested, and instead chose the hospitality business. Thus, his gig at Sandals.

Terry and Jonathan hit it off right away. Jonathan, Terry has said, didn't know she was a famous author. And with that gentle voice, that height that made her feel diminutive and squishy, those big eyes, those sexy lips, and that bronze skin, she was instantly attracted.

Jonathan Plummer had a gentle voice, a gentle manner, good posture, no self-esteem issues. He made eye contact with her, took her out, was affectionate and attentive, and had good manners . . . all ordinary things, but which may have been missing in her previous relationships. "He's so demonstrative and protective," she gushed, "and it feels good having him in my life. He'll just rub me on my head like I'm a little kid, you know, or like if I bump my arm and say 'Ouch,' he'll put his head up against my forehead and his hands on my head and he'll just say 'Hush'. Then he'll put his arms around me, and I mean there's something really comforting about that, and he does it a lot. I'm almost ready to bump into shit on purpose."

For a woman who had no problem striking out on her own, who had no problem defending herself against that which wasn't even attacking her just in case it *might,* who transformed her image from a Plain Jane into a Tantalizing Terry, it would seem like a piece of cake to have enough self-esteem, to think enough of herself, to be able to process an attraction to a man separate and apart from his age (as long as he wasn't a minor!). Yet, Terry had a problem with Plummer's age.

"I couldn't believe I actually liked someone his age," she said. "But of course, men do it all the time."

Anyway, romance was not what she had gone to Jamaica for. "I wasn't looking to get laid. I'm sort of past that age where sex is enough to just lure me, you know? That's when you're in your twenties. It doesn't work like that with me. It's a whole lot of other stuff. But shit happens.

"I started questioning, like why me, why did I meet this young man and we just sort of hit it off? I never in a million years would have dreamed—I've never been out with a younger man before, but I really like him and he likes me, and then I started thinking about this whole double standard that men have been doing this for years and nobody says anything about it, so I said, you know, why not. Feels good.

"He didn't know about any movie or anything, because there was no movie at the time. No, he didn't know who I was. Even when I told him I was a writer. He said, 'That's nice. For magazines?' And I was like, no, books. 'Oh, that's nice.' So it was really refreshing.

"The beauty of dealing with Jonathan is that he didn't even know who I was, and he didn't even care. He's so untarnished that all he knew was that he liked me. And even after he found out who I was, he still liked me. It was great to meet someone who wasn't intimidated by me. But even when he found out that I was really well known and had quite a bit of money he didn't change the way he acted."

Terry couldn't contain herself, and called Deborah Schindler from Jamaica to tell her about Jonathan. It seemed as if Terry was in awe that someone could love her, that she deserved to be loved.

"As I was walking along the beach, I said, 'Mama, you did this, didn't you?' " she remembered. 'I think my mother said, 'It's time.'

"I examined myself to see whether the feelings were real. The way I felt when I was leaving Jamaica was a lot different from the way I was feeling when I was arriving. When I did an honest appraisal of the causes of the changes, I felt that I had to include Jonathan along with the therapeutic sun, fresh air, water—I love to hear it— and the sand. I felt so good, and I didn't want to ignore that."

When Terry returned home, her friends could tell that something was up as soon as they saw her face. Their reaction, she said, was " 'Terry, girl, you better go get that man. Send that motherfucker a ticket. Get his ass up here 'cause we ain't seen you look like this in years. Fuck what anybody else says, 'cause, girl, this is your life.'

"My three sisters each had a different reaction to the 'real source' of my happiness. I told them the full story. One said no to the relationship. The other was cool about it. The third went along with me.

"Some people have said I've gone soft," she said later. "So finding love means going soft? Who cares? I found some happiness, and who knows how long it will last, but I am going to enjoy it while it does."

And in typical Terry fashion, she had to get it out: on paper. "I met a younger man and things just changed and I sort of had to reassess, emotionally, what had happened to me. Gradually I started feeling like myself again, and ended up writing a book about how you lose your spirit and what you have to give up to get it back."

Terry turned the memories of her Jamaica interlude into a novel, which she wrote in a flash, a mere three weeks, beginning on September 6, and completing the first draft on September 30. "She would read me excerpts as she was writing it," Deborah Schindler said in an interview. "I was tickled that she read from her book for me."

Terry told her story in the voice of the main character, Stella Payne. Stella is a forty-two-year-old investment analyst and divorced mother of eleven-year-old Quincy. A bionic woman, she does it all and does it well, having amassed the material trappings of a high-income woman: a house, a BMW, a personal trainer. She is happy. No problem, she has everything. But when her son goes away with his dad, leaving Stella free for a few weeks, she takes off—alone—for the Caribbean, for a little vacation at a luxury resort. Within hours, she meets the six foot four Winston Shakespeare (who has Jonathan Plummer's height, some of his mannerisms, and physical characteristics) and is hooked. And of course, Winston is half her age. Stella has to make a decision about how to handle this new lover and what to do with her own life.

Viking Penguin, Terry's publisher, was expecting *A Day Late and a Dollar Short,* but instead got a manuscript called *How Stella Got Her Groove Back.*

But they paid for it: Terry received a seven-figure advance for *Stella.* (Later, appearing on a panel at the Medgar Evers College black writers conference, she told the gathering that she was now paid six million dollars per book.) The book was set for May publication, with a first printing of 800,000 copies in hard-cover—unheard of for a novel written by an African American author and a far cry from that 5,000 first printing that *Mama* had gotten! And by the time *Stella* came out, *Mama* had been re-printed as a mass market paperback—with art by Synthia St. James on the cover, depicting a mother and five children. And Terry's name was in letters twice as high as those of the book's title!

Karmically speaking, it is interesting to note here a parallel be-tween the lives of Terry McMillan and Zora Neale Hurston: Both created literature as a tool to reflect what was going on in their lives. According to her biographer Robert Hemenway, Hurston wrote the novel *Their Eyes Were Watching God* in seven weeks after an "enchanted" visit to Haiti during which she found a "peace I have never known anywhere else on earth." In the novel, Janie Crawford, Hurston's main character, rec-ognizes and celebrates her own wanderlust from birth through her search—through three marriages—for a man who can make her feel whole and fullfilled. (This imagery was described through young Janie's observation of a bee pollinating a bloom

on a pear tree, and Janie wanting to be that bloom, began searching for the bee who could do that to her, so to speak.)

Their Eyes Were Watching God, Hemenway explains, was inspired by Hurston's affair (although at home rather than in the
Caribbean) with a West Indian student, and it was this lover
who was the basis for the novel's character Tea Cake. Tea Cake
turns out to be the man the main character Janie finally chooses
as her true love (or groove, to use a Terry-ism) after unfulfilling
marriages to Logan Killicks (for financial reasons only) and Joe
Starks (for his ambition). It was one of Zora Neale Hurston's
novels that Terry McMillan admired.

(Perhaps if it were written now it would be called *How Janie
Got Her Bee Back?*)

Once the manuscript for *Stella* was submitted, Terry reached
back to the Caribbean and fetched her lover man to Danville,
California, where he moved into the house with Terry, Solomon, and their dog, Timber, in October 1995. Terry was then
in the process of having a house custom built in Danville. In an
interview, she says that she expressed skepticism about the
chances of them being together forever.

When Jonathan first arrived in America, Terry did some
things for him that would make it easier for him to live there.
"When I got paid a gazillion bucks for writing *Stella* . . . I felt
like he should share in the cash," she said, "because without him
I would never have written it. I just gave him a token, which
just blew his mind. He sent it back to Jamaica and invested it,
but he lives off some of it and helps me pay bills."

In the country on a student visa ("He can't legally get a job in the States, especially at his age and he has no real skill," Terry pointed out), Jonathan enrolled at the local public community college, Diablo Valley College, to take courses in hotel management.

Sometimes Terry's maternal instinct was directed toward her lover. "I've tried to encourage Jonathan to have friends his own age. He likes my world, but at the same time I have to encourage him to have his own friends. Most of those friends are like, twenty-two, twenty-three, or nineteen. Sometimes they'll go out together and he'll invite me and I'll say, 'No, I don't think so.' "

And then, while her manuscript of *How Stella Got Her Groove Back* was being transformed into a book, *Waiting to Exhale,* the movie, opened nationwide on December 22, 1995—Christmas weekend.

Just as fans had lined up to buy the book on the day it was released, they lined up to see the movie the weekend it was released. Women of all races could identify with the women in the story. People from all walks of life went to see the movie, providing even more exposure to Terry's work. The film quickly became number one at the box office, ultimately grossing $67 million. Hollywood was flabbergasted: This had never happened before. The top theater earner in the nation was in Los Angeles, California, at the Magic Johnson Theaters in the Baldwin Hills Crenshaw Mall, which showed the film on six sold-out screens. As an added bonus, the soundtrack hit number one on the music charts as well.

Alice Walker even had a comment, published in the online magazine *Salon.* In an interview with her former Spelman College professor Howard Zinn, when asked what she thought of the film *Waiting to Exhale,* she answered "I enjoyed it, although I found the women (in the movie) very strange. I don't think I know any women who are that desperate for men. But I have inquired among people that I meet, and they say there are women who are really that desperate. In a way it hurts me, because I feel like the world is full of abundance, in relationships as well as in other areas, and to be fixated on any person or thing is just not good for your soul.

"Whether or not Terry McMillan should have written this or made a movie of it or whatever—of course she should have. This is how she sees life. She is an artist and she should be supported in her view. I hope that people are more understanding and less eager to trash than they were ten years ago."

Representing the professional critics, Roger Ebert's opinion was that whereas *The Joy Luck Club* "was high drama, this film is middlebrow, in which the women face not war, famine, and firing squads, but cheaters, liars, dopers, and guys who look fine but turn out to be gay . . . *Waiting to Exhale* is not really an assault on black men (and men in general), but an escapist fantasy that women in the audience can enjoy by musing, 'I wish I had her problems', and her car, house, wardrobe, figure, and men, even wrong men."

In the *Hollywood Reporter* Duane Byrge called the film a "warm story of sisterly survival" with "a terrific ensemble cast . . . this vibrant, bittersweet film will touch home with adults across the board who have experienced frustration in finding a mate."

Susan Stark, the *Detroit News* film critic, assured her readers that the women characters were strong and successful: "You will not confuse them with girlz 'n the hood . . . for all the pleasure there is in seeing effective, great-looking black women grappling with major life issues on screen, *Waiting to Exhale* is an uneven piece. It's a movie that drifts along from one fine moment to another, but it has no real drive and no discernible rhythm. Inevitably, that diminishes its impact."

Los Angeles Times film critic Kenneth Turan felt that the movie was "a pleasant if undemanding piece of work . . . *Waiting to Exhale* is easy listening for the eyes if you're in the mood and aren't too demanding. A good man may or may not be hard to find, but the films about the search will always find an audience."

Jack Matthews echoed this in *Newsday* when he wrote "Many men, it will come as no surprise to many women, are lousy lovers. But few could be any lousier than the self-gratifying, attention-deficit-disordered, slam-bam, thank you ma'am, 'Was it as good for you as it was for me?' bozos who appeared in Terry McMillan's best-selling novel *Waiting to Exhale,* and who are riotously reprised in Forest Whitaker's filmed adaptation."

The headline of Stephen Hunter's comments for the *Baltimore Sun* read, "For Men, *Waiting to Exhale* Would Be Hard to Swallow If It Were Not So Funny." In it, Hunter stated that the film was "colossally entertaining but darkly bitter . . . angry, corrosive and nasty . . . America, according to McMillan, doesn't suffer a bastard shortage. If only it weren't so darned amusing, it would be pretty tough to get through. . . . But it's an enchantment: bitter yet mesmerizing and marginally hopeful."

In the *Boston Globe,* Jay Carr referred to the movie as "both a throwback to the glossy women's film of Hollywood's glory days and a smart contemporary screenful of black sensibility."

For the "Teen Scene" section of the *Boston Herald* movie review, young Millie Commodore felt that the movie "sheds a positive light on women and shows that women don't need to depend on men if they have friends. I would definitely recommend this movie for women who think there's no hope or that their lives are falling apart. *Waiting to Exhale* shows audiences that if they just have faith in themselves, things will work out."

Tracie Reddick, writing in the *Tampa Tribune,* exhaled herself about the fact that *"Exhale* is a hilarious, feel-good dramedy that provides a refreshing change from the recent trend of shoot-'em-up, drug-dealing films that primarily show black women in a negative light."

Once again, it was time to give interviews about *Waiting to Exhale,* the movie. Terry was hounded for interviews.

"A lot of people have misread this film. They think it's about women trying to find Mr. Right. I see it as the opposite: What happens when all you look for is someone, and they always are Mr. Wrong because you don't really discriminate.

"It struck a chord, emotionally, because women are basically saying, we just want to be treated a little better—with a little more tenderness and care.

"What I do with black men in this film, in particular, is sort of parody the lovemaking scenes. That's why they're funny . . . because in almost every film you see with male leads, the males, from Arnold on down, are always studs. They are always full of sexual vigor, and they're just dynamic lovers. Not once have you ever seen a woman jump up from 007 and say, 'That wasn't all I thought it was going to be.' They're always dynamic lovers.

"There are going to be more films about the African American middle class now that Hollywood knows we are basically very proud to see ourselves portrayed in a more realistic light. All of us don't live in the 'hood. All of us don't carry guns and gang-bang and live in the projects, barefoot and pregnant and uneducated.

"The part that I really have a problem with is the whole notion of division. That really disturbs me. Just like at a lot of these *Waiting to Exhale* parties, at which the women all get together. I can't understand why they won't take their boyfriends, or husbands, or brothers . . . I understand the whole notion of sisterhood, and nobody feels stronger about it than I do, but it just seems that would be a great place to bond with the guys.

"Intelligent people know you don't write a book or film and say that this is how all people behave, that all black men are poor lovers, or that all black men love white women, all black women burn up their husband's stuff after they say they're leaving them."

In January 1996, another member of the McMillan family showed her talents too.

Arriving in bookstores that month was Rosalyn McMillan's *Knowing,* a novel set in Detroit with a plot based on Rosalyn's life. Its main character is Ginger Montgomery, an attractive, intelligent factory worker with a supportive husband, four beautiful children, and a fabulous home—who decides to pursue an education and a better career.

"It's a common dilemma of modern life," Rosalyn said in an interview with her hometown newspaper in Port Huron. "How can (a woman) balance the ties and responsibilities of a family with the need to nurture the self? I consider it a contemporary romance . . . a coming of age of a middle-class African American female who changes her life."

For over twenty years, Rosalyn—like her character Ginger—had worked for the Ford Motor Company. Getting up at three-thirty every morning, she would drive for forty-five minutes to her job as a sewing machine operator, sewing car seat cushions for Lincoln Continentals. "My mama cried when I went into that factory," Rosalyn said. "She didn't raise any of us to do that. She intended for all of us to go to college. But I got married right out of high school and went to work."

Because she was fast, Rosalyn made good money, sometimes up to $1,200 a week. "Factory work can be really satisfying if you look at it for the monetary value. But eventually . . . I felt like I was cheating my children because I was tired all the time. I wanted more but wasn't sure what to do about it." To solve that problem, she started various businesses—including makeup, tailoring, bridal dresses, jewelry—but since she was still working at the factory, she couldn't devote sufficient time to anything, and the businesses all failed.

In 1989, after two car accidents, she developed chronic back pain that ended her days of lifting those twenty-pound seat cushions. "I had two choices: to work in continuous pain, or start a new career." In 1992, she took a medical retirement from the factory.

The new career turned out to be writing, inspired by a conversation with her sister Terry, who mentioned that in 1991, only thirteen novels were published by black authors, including her own book, *Waiting to Exhale.* "When she told me that, it kind of blew me away. Then I got to thinking, I can do that."

Well, almost. Completely without writing experience, Rosalyn had a long way to go. And she didn't want Terry's help; she wanted to do it all on her own. In a concentrated version of Terry's experience, Rosalyn took writing classes, attended writing seminars, formed a writer's group, joined the organization Romance Writers of America, and spent hours at her local public library in Southfield, Michigan. The original version of the manuscript took her a year to write; after she submitted it, it took another year for her to write a satisfactory revision. All together, she said, she rewrote the book five times and wore out two computers. Now and then, Terry checked up on the progress: "She'd call and ask, 'How's the book going, Booge?' " said Rosalyn. "I'd let her know I was working on it, then she'd let me go on my merry way."

Throughout the book, Rosalyn, too, stuck to the Write-What-You-Know rule: Detroit locations (the Renaissance Center, Belle Isle, the Whitney Restaurant) are liberally mentioned.

Ginger's mother, Katherine, was inspired by Madeline (and given her middle name). Ginger's father, Lewis, was given Rosalyn's father's middle name. Chapter titles were taken from popular Motown hit songs like "You're My Everything," "Where Did Our Love Go?" "Ain't Too Proud to Beg," "Since I lost My Baby," and "Sexual Healing." And Rosalyn gave the character Ginger alopecia, a medical condition causing periodic hair loss that Rosalyn has suffered from since age eighteen. "I wanted women to see that you don't have to close yourself in a shell and stop living because of it."

When it was time to find an agent, Rosalyn contacted Denise Stinson, a black literary agent based in Detroit. Stinson didn't recognize the last name at first. "McMillan's a fairly common name, so the connection never occurred to me," Stinson said. But she did use the name as a negotiating point, and scored a five-figure deal with Warner Books to publish the hardcover edition. Following publication, Rosalyn went off on a six-city reading tour, and *Knowing* would become a national bestseller.

Rosalyn would later write *One Better,* published in 1997. *One Better* is the story of Spice Witherspoon, an affluent Detroit community leader and restaurant owner. Spice, who is a widow with two self-destructive adult daughters named Mink and Sterling, seeks the right someone to share her life with. And *Blue Collar Blues,* published in 1998, was Rosalyn's novel of the lives and loves of workers in a Detroit auto plant—amid tensions caused by competition between workers, the outsourcing of jobs to Mexico, and the impending secret sale of the plant.

....

As for Terry's book *How Stella Got Her Groove Back*, Deborah Schindler had read the manuscript months before publication, and approached Terry about bringing the new story to the screen. "I felt so connected to Terry and her material on both *Exhale* and *Stella*," Schindler said. "Her characters are funny, sad, and realistic people. And nobody writes dialogue better than Terry McMillan."

Schindler took the finished *Stella* manuscript to studio execs, and in early March of 1996, Twentieth Century Fox production president Tom Rothman acquired the screen rights to *Stella* for what sources familiar with the deal estimated at $1.5 million, obviously hoping that it would have the same kind of success as *Waiting to Exhale*.

"There was a lot of competition for it," Rothman said after the deal was completed. "We are thrilled for two reasons: one, it is a great, dynamic piece of material and chock-full with great moments; and two, it continues a very successful partnership between McMillan and Fox."

In April, Fox again signed Ron Bass to collaborate with Terry on writing the screenplay, and Deborah Schindler was chosen again to produce. Schindler, now head of her own production company, Deborah Schindler Productions, had earned Hollywood's respect by making Terry's books into movies and delivering a previously untapped audience—black women.

Waiting to Exhale was still riding a wave of success. At the 27th annual NAACP Image Awards (which honor people and organizations who portray blacks positively in the arts), it won the award for Outstanding Film of 1995. Angela Bassett was named Outstanding Actress, Loretta Devine, Outstanding Supporting Actress, and the soundtrack won the awards for soundtrack and album. Whitney Houston's performance of the movie's theme song, "Exhale (Shoop Shoop)" earned the award for female recording artist.

By the spring of 1996, Terry's new house was ready, and she, Solomon, and Jonathan moved in. It was a four-bedroom home, with pool, sauna, and Jacuzzi, decorated in bright colors (such as teal, purple, chartreuse, and mustard) and leather tile. Jonathan's passion for lovebirds had been indulged, for there were thirteen of them in the house. Terry had a servant, finally, a houseman named Ali.

How Stella Got Her Groove Back was published on Monday, April 29, 1996. On that morning, women lined up at bookstores to buy *Groove* as soon as it went on sale. The hardcover's $23 price tag did not discourage Terry's fans at all from buying the book with the collage-type cover of a woman in a straw hat, arms upraised, standing on an elegant patio, and being watched by a tall man in the background.

"It's a real photo, you know," explained Terry. "I actually met a couple who was married at that hotel, the Jamaica Palace." On the back cover was a photo of Terry, hair piled on top of her head and cascading down to her shoulder in curls, satin blouse buttoned up to her neck. There was a rare smile on her face, and it suggested that she was pleased about something.

The biggest surprise in *Stella* was the preponderance of long sentences without punctuation. Or as Terry says some readers asked her, "Girl, did you miss that week in school on punctuation?" Not at all, she explained. "It is reflective of my stream of consciousness, which has no punctuation.

"I knew that it would be jarring at first. But I expected the readers to join in my mental and emotional tirade, which does not express exhaustion, but exhilaration instead."

There was another tour—but this time, Terry was not alone. Jonathan was there with her, for the fans to scrutinize, appreciate, or criticize, patiently waiting (and signing copies of *Stella,* too) while eager fans surrounded Terry. Since *Waiting to Exhale,* her book signings had to have a strategy, because there are only so many books one person can sign. At some events, the number of books she would sign was limited to one, or she would give nameplates or preautographed photos instead of signing. Sometimes the coordinators of the events provided a hand masseuse for her and coffee for the fans on line.

The book's release and Terry's visibility marked the first time her fans heard about Jonathan, but the two had in fact been together for almost a year when the book was released in April. Once the readers made the connection, the first reaction of many was that she had gone down there and met herself a poor, struggling, unrefined native, or perhaps a hired lover, because that was the only action she could get. Her sharp response was, "I can get a man, I don't need Jonathan to rock my world, 'cuz I can get my world rocked anytime I like."

After the book tour, Terry and Jonathan went to Jamaica (a reading was scheduled there, too!) and a little vacation. Or, as she said, "This time, I'm taking my groove with me."

Reviews of the book included Sarah Ferguson's *New York*

Times Book Review account, which called the book's "message as uncomplicated as a glass of fresh-squeezed papaya juice: If aging men can rev their engines with pretty young trophy wives, why can't middle-aged women treat themselves to dreamy, dishy toy boys?"

John Skow, in *Time* magazine, called the book "a silly wish-fulfillment fantasy that barely qualifies as beach literature . . . It's a dubious sort of good luck that the publication of her slightest and fluffiest novel has brought McMillan her greatest reward . . . Most of the time her chapters, though they can rank nearly as high as [Danielle] Steel's and [Judith] Krantz's in breathy descriptions of dressing, undressing, and furniture, have a brassy realism that saves them from the trash bin."

In *Library Journal,* Corinne O. Nelson wrote that "Nothing here convinces the reader that the island is an exotic vacation spot; McMillan's valiant attempts at describing the countryside are weak, and even Stella's choice of meals consists exclusively of pasta."

Readers either loved the book or hated it. (One of the people who didn't read it was Solomon Welch. "I want to, but my mom won't let me," he told Barbara Walters in a televised interview. "She says it's kind of X-rated, that there's lots of profanity and sex and she doesn't really want me to read it yet." When Walters asked if he would try to sneak the book away and read it, he assured her that he wouldn't.)

Numerous readers recommended the book to their divorced

and separated sisters. Some shared it with their children, opening up an opportunity to discuss adult relationships. As for that stream-of-consciousness language, some said that the flow kept them interested, and made perfect sense, especially since the story was told in first person. Once again, many commented on how they could relate to the many personal situations; they had to acknowledge that the theme was universal, one that all women (and men) could identify with.

Of course, there were complaints that her book (like her others, of course) was merely confirmation that all black men are dogs, and that to look for intellectual stimulation in one of her books was a waste of time. Perceptive readers suggested that now that she was in love, her tone would mellow out, and that they were glad that she'd found happiness.

And one more thing: The phrase "get your groove back" became common usage.

The biggest reaction of all was from black women who were inspired to take more control of their lives—and for some, that meant packing their swimsuits, toothbrushes, and a few condoms, and flying down to Jamaica "to get my GROOVE on!" Or, as Ishmael Reed quipped a while later, "These women are bringing so many Jamaican guys back here it's almost like *Amistad!*" referring to the slave ship on which hundreds of strong black bodies were transported to America, and which had been the topic of a recent movie.

In the meantime, work was progressing on the *Stella* movie. Terry and Ron Bass worked on the script in that same teamwork style that had paid off on *Waiting to Exhale*. After they had finished the first draft of the script, though, they weren't happy with it.

"We asked five potential directors to come in with improvements they thought the script needed, and four of them really didn't see any changes that needed to be made," Terry said in an interview. "We knew different. We were having problems making this work."

The only candidate who acknowledged that their screenplay was lacking was Kevin Rodney Sullivan, a former actor (*More American Graffiti, Night Shift,* and TV's *Happy Days*), whose directing experience had been limited to television projects such as the HBO movie *Soul of the Game.*

"I felt it was a beautiful inner journey," Sullivan said, "but it would have been difficult to build scenes or drama out of something going on in someone's head. There's an intriguing character from Stella's past, a best friend named Delilah, who's just sort of mentioned in the book. I thought it was important to put Delilah in the movie so that Stella would have someone to talk and interact with. That would help to pull the story out of Stella's head. Her relationship with Delilah adds a whole new depth to the story."

The draft was rewritten, and in the revised version, Stella went to Jamaica not alone, but with the warm, wild and wacky Delilah—who of course represents Doris Jean Austin, Terry's real-life best friend. In the book, Stella's story is told in the character's own voice, through stream of consciousness and internal dialogue. But with Delilah added as a character, the conversations between Stella and Delilah could express the inner thoughts that in the book, Stella had in private. When the team found out that Whoopi Goldberg was interested in the role of Delilah, it enabled them to have more fun with the writing. For one, it allowed Terry and Ron to write about friendship, which was, Sullivan noted, "something they do extraordinarily well. Terry's unique voice is best expressed through the relationships between women."

And then there was the character Winston Shakespeare, who is depicted entirely from Stella's viewpoint in the book. Sullivan said, "We worked on making Winston three dimensional, so the audience would have some sense of him as a man, and his relationship with Stella would be a viable one. While there are many reasons for her not to be with him, we had to understand why she could not turn away from her feelings—why it was so right even if the circumstances were wrong."

Visually, Sullivan used camera movements to convey Stella's strong qualities: "The shots are compressed," he explained, "lending the feeling that she is large and the world is small. The camera is always moving, and the scenes have a lot of energy." Then when she arrives in Jamaica, her view opens up, and so does the cinematography: "We used wide lenses to give an enhanced depth of field. The color is rich, the image is sharp, and the actors move within wide frames. Stella gets perspective; the world is big."

Waiting to Exhale veteran Angela Bassett was cast as Stella. "I haven't seen her soft in a lot of movies she is in," said Terry, "and I thought she might appreciate being softer on screen, and feel good, and be in love. We don't get that many opportunities, especially at forty years old."

Other main cast members were twenty-year-old newcomer Taye Diggs as Winston, Whoopi Goldberg as Delilah, and Michael J. Pagan as Stella's son Quincy. The movie was shot in southern California (masquerading as the San Francisco Bay Area and New York) and on the island of Jamaica. The production spent four weeks in Montego Bay capturing the lush tropical paradise, and over 150 Jamaicans were hired in cast and crew positions: former Miss World Lisa Hanna and local actress Denise Hunt had speaking roles, and other well-known Jamaican personalities filled in as extras. Taye Diggs, who was born in New Jersey, was taught to speak in a Jamaican accent by dialect coach Jerome Butler.

In May 1996, *Time* magazine published an interview with Terry. On the subject of Jonathan, her thoughts were, "I don't anticipate us being together for the rest of my life, but right now it works and it's good for him and it works for me and I don't care what anybody thinks . . . men have done this shit for years. Nobody ever says anything about them and they marry chicks young enough to be their daughters."

A year after they moved in together, Jonathan and Terry were still together in their big house in Danville. Terry acknowledged that Jonathan was good with Solomon, which of course was important to her. And Solomon liked him, as he told Barbara Walters: "I was pretty excited [about Jonathan coming to live here] because I never really had a dad to live with and so after

Jonathan comes, he feels kind of like my dad or uncle or brother, you know? It's kind of fun."

Terry also acknowledged, "I'm not the easiest person to live with, and I have to give him credit because he's hung in there."

That fall, Terry exclusively revealed to Dionne St. Hill, a journalist for *The Voice*, a British newspaper, that marriage might be in the works. "Jonathan asked me to marry him," Terry confessed, "while we were in Jamaica this summer. Unless something really weird happens or I get cold feet, we'll probably get married in December."

Things were going so well that Terry was considering having another baby while she was still biologically able. Reportedly, a discussion on this subject arose when she mentioned to Jonathan that she was considering having her tubes tied. Jonathan's reply was that he didn't think she should do that just yet. A short time afterward, she received a numerology reading. Its prediction? You might have a baby this year. "If I had a child now, I would be its grandmother," she said in an interview. "It would come out and say, 'Hi granny!' "

And as journalist Ros Davidson wrote in an article in one of Scotland's Sunday newspapers, "She reveals she had a breast 'lift' in July. 'They were just drooping and getting on my nerves,' she adds with hilarious and reflexive bluntness, glancing down at her too-tight blouse."

At times, though, most of Terry's interviews sounded as if she was seriously reverting into that defensive mode where Jonathan was concerned. Consider the *Daily Telegraph* article, in which reporter Michael Shelden noted, "Plummer is now undergoing what might be called 'boyfriend boot camp.' Apparently, he is not always a model pupil, and she has warned him that there is a limit to her patience. If he continually disappoints her and shows that he does not want to please her, she will cut him loose without a second thought. She has said to him: 'Have you ever had a surprise attack, like the one you've seen in those movies? That's what this will be like. When I get tired, all I'll say is, "get your stuff," and if you're not here, I'll just take it and put it on the steps.' "

In his article, Shelden perceptively noted that Terry's clever writing helps to hide the anger inside—the type of anger carried by someone who has been "burnt once too often," he wrote. "If anyone is going to be burnt again, she is not going to be the victim."

In 1996, Terry made her first trip to the new South Africa. In an interview published in *Ebony* magazine, she said that she and Plummer were happy at the moment, but that she didn't expect the relationship to last. "Initially," she said, "we both had a feeling of forever. We experienced the eroticism and excitement of new love. Later, though, there was a difference. We see the world differently. He's growing up."

The fame continued, but Terry was wearing down. She had enough money to enable her to choose—and in turn, reject—among projects that were offered to her. *Stella,* she stated, would be the last novel she would adapt for the screen, no matter how much money she was offered.

In December 1997, the film of *How Stella Got Her Groove Back* was completed. The film opened nationwide on August 14, 1998, to positive reviews (Taye Diggs's body "had both the women in the movie and in the audience swooning," said one). Audiences loved it, calling it a "feel-good movie," and many saw it more than once. It would go on to gross over $37 million.

The film's soundtrack, produced by R & B's Jimmy Jam and Terry Lewis, was a mix of hip hop, R & B, and reggae. Original tunes were performed by Big Punisher and Beenie Man, Mary J. Blige, Kevin Ford, Wyclef Jean, Diana King, Maxi Priest, Shaggy, Soul II Soul, with "Your Home Is in My Heart (Stella's Love Theme)" performed by Boyz II Men featuring Chante Moore.

Most reviews noted that the movie was a little on the fluffy side, a bit unbelievable, but admitted that the slick, polished production was good for the eyes. Some critics compared it to the 1973 movie *Forty Carats,* in which Liv Ullman played a forty-year-old successful businesswoman who is romanced, while vacationing in Greece, by a twenty-two-year-old man (Edward Albert, Jr.).

Critic Gene Siskel wrote, "What are we supposed to think? If you can find a great-looking mate, life will be more beautiful? Who wrote this screenplay, the Jamaican Tourist Board? Looking at two beautiful people for close to two hours is easy on the eyes; unfortunately, however, there is nothing in *Stella* to stimulate what's behind the eyes."

In the *New York Times,* Stephen Holden wrote that the movie "may be the first to blatantly portray a tropical paradise as a sexual mecca beckoning tired American businesswomen to shed their clothes and inhibitions and roll around with the local talent . . . the movie [has] the flavor of a Chippendales-in-the-Caribbean promotion."

In *Variety,* Todd McCarthy wrote that "Lustrous production values are designed to enhance the world of extreme privilege inhabited by the characters."

Another reviewer noted that *Stella* was much kinder to men than *Waiting to Exhale.*

And Terry McMillan said, "I am pleased with what I have seen cinematically. It is beautiful. I think there's the joy he brings her, and the comfort he offers her, and how his income and social status don't play a large role. Years ago that is the way it used to be. People became friends for who they are, not what they have, and it has been lost big time."

Haitian Americans were offended by one line in the movie. In the film, Bassett's character is asked by her sister if she fears getting AIDS in Jamaica. Another sister interrupts saying, "No, that's Haiti, Miss Manners."

In response, Haitian Americans and Haitian government officials criticized the movie, saying that that line linking their country with the AIDS crisis was an unwarranted slur.

"We deplore that this company [Twentieth Century Fox] could say such a thing," said Dr. Michaele Amedee-Gedeon, general director of Haiti's Ministry of Health. "We accuse them of ignorance and judgment without proof." Officials at Haiti's Ministry of Tourism also spoke out against the movie, and Haitian American groups, complaining that the statement revives an old, unfair stereotype, staged protests against the movie in front of the Twentieth Century Fox offices in New York.

Haitian singer Wyclef Jean, who appeared on the movie's soundtrack, said later that he was "saddened and offended to see my country used as a brunt for an AIDS joke in the movie. AIDS is a crisis and not a comedy."

Subsequently, Twentieth Century Fox released a statement: "It has been brought to our attention that a line of dialogue in *How Stella Got Her Groove Back* was found to be insensitive and troubling to many people in the Haitian community. Although the line was true to the character, we do understand the insensitivity of her remark and apologize for any distress it has caused. As a result, we have decided to delete this line from the home video version of the film."

Indeed, Terry McMillan had come a long way from Port Huron—just by writing.

Ever restless, between novels Terry continued to write, speak, and make public appearances, sometimes giving readings from her still-in-progress novel *A Day Late and a Dollar Short* (which she describes as a story about "siblings dealing with loss and forgiveness, rivalry, love, jealousy, and missed opportunity").

In the spring of 1998, at the third annual *Los Angeles Times* Festival of Books at UCLA in California, Terry acknowledged the positive changes for black writers of commercial works. For example, a decade ago, "Black writers did not go on book tours. But that has changed." As had the world of movies, because *Waiting to Exhale* "was one of the first movies about African

American women who were not downtrodden." Industry insiders "didn't know it was going to do as well as it did. But they were shocked about *Titanic* too."

But Terry's feeling was that too many black-authored books were being compared to *Waiting to Exhale*. She told an interviewer:

"I'm so sick of *Waiting to Exhale*. They act like that was the only book ever written. Why does everything have to be compared to that book?

"Everybody was giving myself and the book credit for opening up doors in the publishing industry for African American writers. Then the movie supposedly did that for movies. Spike Lee had already done that. I was excited about what *Waiting to Exhale* offered. But what appears to have happened is that there are so many books being published . . . that are really bad books.

"I'm not trying to knock some folks, and I'm not trying to put myself up on a pedestal, but a lot of people are writing books because they think they can."

Here, you can just see Terry putting on her writing instructor's hat when she continues, "If the work doesn't resonate, if it doesn't make you stop and think, it's Teflon fiction. After you read it you forget about it.

"They're writing for shock value. They're unoriginal. And everybody is trying to imitate somebody else. And if I read one more story about four women . . ."

She blames this flood of mediocre books partly on the publishers, comparing them to filmmakers during the "blaxploitation" film years.

"These books have no editing. There is grammatically poor writing, grave errors, and things that don't make sense. I guess the editors think that black people are too stupid to know the difference, that we don't know the difference between good and bad writing. There's gratuitous sex and profanity in every other sentence."

Looking back on it, this is how Terry sees it: "I was paid a lot of money. And that is where *Waiting to Exhale* has gotten too much credit. People started thinking, 'Hey, you can get rich by writing a book.' It wasn't a story that motivated them. It was the money and that is a sad-assed reason to write a novel.

"I've gotten a lot of money because God was on my side. I didn't know any famous writers when I started writing. I wanted to tell stories. I could have taught and paid the rent."

In June 1998, Terry's mentor Ishmael Reed was one of twenty-nine people selected as a John D. and Catherine T. MacArthur Foundation fellow (the designation is informally known as the MacArthur Award). Every summer since 1981, the foundation has been presenting the awards to honor outstanding creativity—with no strings attached. There is no application process: A secret panel of one hundred anonymous scouts, selected annually, look for likely fellows, then write letters of nomination to the foundation's board, which makes the final choice of twenty to forty award recipients. Some of the winners are famous, some of them unknown, but their prize is an unrestricted five-year grant, ranging from $150,000 to $350,000, to be used for any purpose they desire.

Reed, who received the maximum award, said that he would use some of it to stage a San Francisco production of his opera, *Gethsemane Park.*

The director of the MacArthur Fellows Program was Catharine Stimpson, who had been a panelist with Terry for the 1990 National Book Awards, and who had been appointed to the MacArthur Foundation in 1994. Stimpson has said that she has little influence over who becomes a MacArthur Fellow, although she once told a reporter for the *Chicago Tribune* that "one of my responsibilities is to make sure activists are as much represented as academics." The fellowships are often also called genius grants, a term Stimpson said was invented "by the media and by the public at the very beginning of the program."

"I still can't believe it," Reed said of his award. "I had no idea."

Terry told reporters, "It's about time he got one. He's brilliant. He was very supportive of young writers, and they don't forget him."

And her romance with Jonathan seemed to still be going strong. "He has forced me to slow down," she said, "and to take two hours in the middle of the day to read a book and not feel guilty about it. He'll say, 'Terry, forget about the laundry. Forget about cooking. Let's go out to dinner, let's go for a walk.' He braids my hair. He's not intimidated by me in the least. He's very, very open.

"For me, part of the beauty of it is, I've been given an opportunity to look at things a second time that I either glossed over or overlooked or was moving too fast to pay attention to. It's kinda nice."

In September 1998, Terry was invited to be a speaker at the annual Maui Writers Conference in Hawaii. At the conference, both aspiring and professional writers can meet and learn from best-selling authors, award-winning journalists, editors, agents, and publishers. The host hotel was the plush Grand Wailea Resort, Hotel & Spa, a five-wing structure with 761 guest rooms, located on a forty acre site on Maui's south shore. Terry, who was there with Jonathan and Solomon, enjoyed the gardens, international art collection, restaurants, children's facilities, and world-class spa.

Her presentation was for Sunday, September 6, from 7:00 P.M. to 7:45 P.M., and her topic was "Get in the Groove," wherein she would tell her story and give tips on how she had mastered the demanding life of a celebrated author and screenwriter. "The story of Terry's difficult but dedicated rise to stardom will help you get back to your own chosen path," said the conference program.

When Terry made her presentation, it was as Mrs. Jonathan Plummer. On the previous day, September 5, 1998, she had finally married Jonathan Plummer on a nearby Maui beach. Solomon, Terry's sister Crystal, and a niece and nephew watched as a barefoot Terry took her vows. The radiant bride's shoulder-length braids were coiffed into a crown, with a few cascading over her face and shoulders. She wore an ankle-length, cream-colored gauze ensemble, purchased at Neiman Marcus: a simple

dress with spaghetti straps under a matching long-sleeved sheer
gauze duster. Jonathan wore gauze, too: a long-sleeved, see-
through tunic with a deep collar in back, over matching pants.
He had purchased his outfit the year before, but had never worn
it. Terry's small bouquet was a spray of white and pink flowers,
and the whole wedding party wore leis of white flowers around
their necks.

The hotel provided everything required for the nuptials, including the cake, champagne, photographer, and video. For this
service, the couple paid $899, and considered it a great little
party. "We were thinking about doing it again in Jamaica, with
his family," Terry told an interviewer, adding, "We want to get
married every year!" At the time, only two sentences on the
marriage were released to the news media, but one reporter
added knowingly, "Check upcoming novels for details on how
the marriage works out."

If Terry McMillan stops writing tomorrow, her impact on the
world has already been made. She didn't want to make an impact, she just wanted to write. And that is why Terry's biography
is worthy of being written. Like all our biographies, it is the
story of the process we go through in the making of ourselves,
and how that self spreads out to the universe to touch our fellow
beings.

Gerald Stern's poem, "When I Have Reached the Point of
Suffocation," which Terry chose as the inscription for *Mama,*
said:

It takes years to learn how to look at the destruction
of beautiful things;

to learn how to leave the place of oppression;

and how to make your own regeneration
out of nothing.

No one can deny that Terry McMillan is one of those people
who has indeed made her "own regeneration out of nothing."
In other words, when life gives you lemons . . . make lemonade.
And sometimes, novelization is the best revenge.